WOMEN:
ICONS OF CHRIST

PHYLLIS ZAGANO

Paulist Press
New York / Mahwah, NJ

Cover/interior image: painting *Virgin Annunciate* by Antonello da Messina (1476). Photo courtesy of Wikipedia.
Cover and book design by Lynn Else

Library of Congress Cataloging-in-Publication Data
Names: Zagano, Phyllis, author.
Title: Women: icons of Christ / Phyllis Zagano.
Description: New York : Paulist Press, 2020. | Includes bibliographical references. | Summary: "Will the Church restore its past in acceptance of its present and in preparation for its future? Through extensive research into ministry practices of the past, their dismissal, and re-emergence in new forms in our own day, this book envisions a future where the diaconate obtains its full expression to include women"— Provided by publisher.
Identifiers: LCCN 2019043754 (print) | LCCN 2019043755 (ebook) | ISBN 9780809155002 (paperback) | ISBN 9781587688980 (ebook)
Subjects: LCSH: Deaconesses--Catholic Church. | Ordination of women—Catholic Church. | Catholic Church—Clergy.
Classification: LCC BX1912.2 .Z344 2020 (print) | LCC BX1912.2 (ebook) | DDC 262/.142082—dc23
LC record available at https://lccn.loc.gov/2019043754
LC ebook record available at https://lccn.loc.gov/2019043755

ISBN 978-0-8091-5500-2 (paperback)
ISBN 978-1-58768-898-0 (e-book)

Published by Paulist Press
997 Macarthur Boulevard
Mahwah, New Jersey 07430
www.paulistpress.com

Printed and bound in the
United States of America

For Karen M. Doyle, SSJ

CONTENTS

Acknowledgments vii

Introduction xi

1. Baptism.. 1
    Development of the Hierarchy 8
    Phoebe of Romans 16:1 10
    The Women of 1 Timothy 3:11 14
    Acts of the Apostles 6:1–6.. 16

2. Catechesis & Catechisms.. 27
    Catechisms.. 31
    Explaining the Catechism...35
    Women Preaching 44
    Homilies... 45

3. Altar Service 52
    Barred from the Sacred... 56
    Women Are Unclean.. 62
    Clerical Celibacy and Misogyny 65
    Modern Misogyny.. 72

CONTENTS

4. Spiritual Direction & Confession 77

   A Brief History of Spiritual Direction......................................80

   Contemporary Spiritual Direction...82

   Confession...86

   Women's Stories Are Important...93

   Women Deacons and Spiritual Direction 97

   Indulgences...99

5. Anointing of the Sick...101

   Healing and Forgiveness..104

   The Sacrament of the Sick..108

   Deacons and Women in Chaplaincy.......................................113

6. Conclusions..118

ACKNOWLEDGMENTS

NO BOOK JUST HAPPENS. *Women: Icons of Christ* began some years before Pope Francis announced his intention to create a Commission for the Study of the Diaconate of Women, to which he appointed me August 2, 2016. That hot day I first went to the Hofstra University Relations Office, just to let them know, and then to Faculty Computing Services, to thank the many managers and staff there who had helped me with my work and who had taught me so much: Sean Donohue, Alexander Smiros, Jackson Snelling, and Monica Yatsyla come to mind. Surely there were more.

The idea for the book came from conversations with Paulist Press editor Trace Murphy, first at a meeting of the American Academy of Religion, then during a Catholic Theological Society of America convention, later at events at Fordham University, and finally at the Los Angeles Religious Education Congress. Throughout, many members of the Paulist team: Mark-David Janus, CSP, publisher; Bob Byrns, director of marketing and sales; Donna Crilly, senior academic editor; Melene Kubat, administrative assistant and foreign rights manager; Diane Vescovi, senior editor; and many others whom I have never met brought this book to its completion. I thank them each and all.

WOMEN: ICONS OF CHRIST

Beyond Paulist Press, many friends and colleagues helped with the work, and I am especially indebted to Deacon William T. Ditewig, former director of the U.S. Conference of Catholic Bishops' Office for the Diaconate; Gary Macy, Professor of Religious Studies at Santa Clara University; and Carolyn Osiek, RSCJ, professor emerita of New Testament, Brite Divinity School, for their kind assistance on this and other projects during the past few years.

I remain indebted to the generous individuals whose conversations about this topic during the term of the Papal Commission informed my thought: academic colleagues, members of the Commission, friends in the Vatican press corps and Vatican Media, members and staff of the International Union of Superiors General, and library staffs of the Pontifical Gregorian University, Hofstra University, and the Vatican.

My gratitude is unending to the researchers, research assistants, and translators who cheerfully provided assistance over the years: Denver Beattie; Lisa Cathelyn; Colleen Gibson, SSJ; Angela Hollar; Lenin Martell; Carmela Leonforte-Plimack; Jessica Kerber, ACJ; Ivana Mullner; Jacob Rinderknecht; and Cecilia Titizano.

Without question, I could not have done my work without the major assistance of the Conrad N. Hilton Foundation, the Catholic Community Foundation, the Weigand Family Fund, and many generous private donors.

As the work neared completion, I had the joy and honor to receive detailed comments from Paul Crowley, SJ, Jesuit Community Professor at Santa Clara University and editor of *Theological Studies*; and Margaret E. Guider, OSF, associate professor and chair of the ecclesiastical faculty, Boston College School of Theology and Ministry. I remain ever grateful for their suggestions and corrections.

Thanks go as well to my dear friend Irene Kelly, RSHM, who read the completed manuscript. Besides offering good cheer and support along the way, she contributed final corrections.

Karen Doyle, SSJ, to whom this book is gratefully dedicated, has steadfastly stood behind me in the background, cheering me along as I hoped to serve the needs of the Church.

May this work encourage all the women of the Church and of the world to see themselves as icons of Christ, made in the image and likeness of God.

September 3, 2019
Feast of St. Phoebe, Deacon

INTRODUCTION

Wнo CAN BE AN ICON OF CHRIST?

The question haunts me. Documents of the Second Vatican Council teach that all good people who are part of the Church, all good people caught within the net the world calls Christianity, all these good people relying on the exquisite promise of Christ's resurrection are the Body of Christ. It would stand to reason, then, that "all good people" means precisely that. "All good people" means all good men...and women.

Yet, the Catholic Church has excised half its members from the fold. Cut free are all women. How? Women cannot be ordained to church ministry, even though the clearest and most complete church histories include ordained women. What is the argument against ordaining women? The reduction of the complex reasoning is that women do not image Christ. Women cannot symbolize Christ. Women are not icons of Christ.

That is plain wrong. Not only is it wrong, it is a statement that redounds to the most serious and most dangerous views of women around the world. At this writing, there are 2.2 billion Christians—nearly a third of the world's population—living (many suffering) on the Earth, on the planet that Irish poet and Nobel laureate Seamus Heaney once said was in danger of becoming a "dead red berry hung in space."[1] More than half of these Christians hugging our fragile Earth are Catholic Christians of one description or another. They may be Roman Catholics, surely the largest of the Catholic Churches. They may belong to one of the twenty-three other Catholic Churches looking toward Rome for leadership.

But without doubt, half of these people, at least, are female. They are infants, girls, young women, adults, and elderly women of every shape and size, of every color and nationality. These wonderful, beautiful females populate fully half the Catholic Churches—whether Roman or Melkite or Ukrainian or Greek or any other—and they live their entire lives under the cloud of modern Church regulations that decree they cannot be ordained to serve as ministers to the whole Church or even solely to other women. They cannot be ordained because, it is said, they cannot image Christ.

It is a scandal. It is more than a scandal; it is a disfigurement on the entire Body of Christ rendered by those who would deny both history and theology. It goes so deeply against the teachings of the Catholic Churches and against Scripture that it is probably formally heretical.

No matter. The rest of the world seems to have given up the promise of the Gospel for promises of another sort. Jesus, the Christ, is replaced by the god of history, the god of the here and now, to whom the worldly sacrifices of time and money are made.

Do they who say women cannot image Christ understand how they have bent to that god of history? Do they recognize how much they value their own positions and power? Do they understand that every rung they climb on their imagined

---

1. Seamus Heaney, "Verses for a Fordham Commencement," May 23, 1982. See http://fordhamnotes.blogspot.com/2013/08/seamus-heaneys-verses-for-fordham.html (accessed December 10, 2019).

ladder to success is made from the lives of others, mostly women, to whom they have denied full humanity?

Today, the world is erupting with war, hatred, and deceit. In Ukraine, bodies lay untouched and unclaimed for too long from the airplane shot down in a frightening war between groups of peoples who want or do not want to rejoin Russia. In Syria, headless bodies of soldiers lay on the pavement as their severed heads watch from nearby fence posts. In Iraq, Christians live in houses on which large *N*s have been painted, to signify the fact that Nazarenes (an Arabic slur for Christians) live there. In Sudan, in Somalia, in so many other places, Christians live in fear for their livelihoods and too often for their very lives. All Christians—men and women—live this way in these places and in so many other places in the world.

And what about the women?

In too many countries women are denied their full humanity by customs and traditions stuck in medieval mores or worse. In some countries, women cannot vote, drive automobiles, hold jobs or political office, or show their hair or faces or even feet in public. In other countries—in wide swaths of India baking in the searing sun—rape is so common it is barely reported, except when its violence and brutality maims or even kills the bodies of the young and innocent. According to *The Irish Times*, India's National Crime Records Bureau (NCRB) states that 92 women are raped per day in India, reporting 34,651 rapes (or one every twenty-one minutes) in 2015 and nearly a quarter million rapes reported over thirteen years.[2] These are the reported rapes, not the total number. Despite the #MeToo movement, that rape steals a portion

---

2. Sorcha Pollak and Rahul Bedi, "Man Jailed for Seven Years for Raping Irish Woman in India," *The Irish Times*, January 22, 2018, accessed 10/20/19, https://www.irishtimes.com/news/ireland/irish-news/man-jailed-for-seven-years-for-raping-irish-woman-in-india-1.3363933. Also see http://ncrb.gov.in/.

of the soul and brings a living death to so many women is not reported quite so well or widely.

What can the Church do about it? What can the Church do about the fact that women are denied their humanity—their rights, their livelihoods, their freedoms, and, in too many cases, their peace of mind and even their own lives?

Then, think about who can be an icon of Christ. The Vatican and its bureaucrats use pounds of paper arguing for the dignity, even the equality, of all persons. All persons, it says, are made "in the image and likeness of God."

But, the argument goes, women cannot image Christ.

So women cannot be ordained to their historically documented office of deacon because women cannot serve and be *in persona Christi servi*, in the person of Christ the servant.

I do not understand the logic. Perhaps because there is none.

To be clear, I do not argue for women priests. The vocation to priesthood—any vocation really—must be ratified by the whole Church. To perform a sacrament, one must do as the Church does, and the Church does not (that is, the Catholic Churches do not) ordain women as priests and probably never have nor will.

But the Catholic Churches most assuredly have ordained women as deacons, and many theologians, historians, and liturgists attest to this fact. Bishops in the past, Eastern and Western, clearly ordained women as deacons with virtually identical ceremonies to those they used for the men they ordained as deacons.

There are some who argue that the recorded ordinations of women to the diaconate, all permitted by conciliar canons, were not sacramental and that therefore women cannot be sacramentally ordained as deacons today. Such an argument retroactively denies the intent of the ordaining bishops, who clearly knew what they were doing by using virtually identical ceremonies. The argument also denies that women can be ordained, as if the female body is defective matter for the sacrament. The argument makes all sorts of hair-splitting gyrations mostly arguing, for example, that because Phoebe rather than Stephen is invoked in some ordination ceremonies for women, there were separate male and female diaconates. Shall we remember here that Phoebe is the only person in Scripture with the descriptor "deacon" and that Paul did not feminize her title to "deaconess"?[3]

Of course, there was and there is only one diaconate. Yes, male deacons primarily ministered to men, and women deacons primarily ministered to women: women deacons assisted at baptism, catechized women and children, provided spiritual direction to women, heard their confessions, brought them the Eucharist, and anointed them in illness and at death.

Even today, some societies strictly separate men and women. But today, in other societies and other cultures, propriety boundaries are somewhat looser, even as they rise and take effect through preference. That is, women deacons of history ministered to other women and to children. Two questions: (1) Who ministers to women and children today? and (2) Is it impossible to imagine a woman ministering to a man today? The positions and preferences of history and culture are not dispositive for the present; they cannot settle the argument over whether women were sacramentally ordained as deacons in the deep past.

If we admit to the sacramentality of any early ordinations, women were sacramentally ordained. Yet, whether they were sacramentally ordained or not neither proves nor disproves that they can or cannot be sacramentally ordained today. The question is not only about history. Nevertheless, the entire Church—the people of God and the hierarchy—must understand

---

3. διακονος

and accept the history of and a present need for the sacramental ordination of women. It must also understand and accept the fact that the soul enfleshed as female can receive the grace and charism of orders.[4]

To deny sacramental ordination for women as deacons is to deny their full humanity as created in the image and likeness of God. The most simplistic of arguments introduced into the mix is that a woman cannot be ordained as deacon because she cannot be ordained as priest. But the Church teaches women cannot be ordained as priests; it does not teach definitively that women cannot be ordained deacons.

The term "sacred ordination" enters the discussion, possibly but not quite distinguishing the sacred ordination to priesthood and the ministerial ordination of deacon. But does "sacred ordination" mean priestly ordination and only priestly ordination? Are all ordinations priestly ordinations? Is it the sacrament of order or the sacrament of orders? (I leave aside for the present the consecration of bishops, now called an ordination.)

For those who argue the one sacrament of order cannot be separated or received in stages, the diaconate is part of priesthood. For those who argue the sacrament of orders is one, yet able to be distinguished (deacon, priest, bishop), the diaconate stands alone as a separate order not necessarily implying priesthood. One argument against ordained women deacons rests in the teaching that women cannot be priests. The "unicity of order" concept implies that if women cannot be ordained as priests, they therefore cannot be ordained as deacons. (Accepting this argument necessarily accepts its obverse: if women in the ancient Church were ordained as

---

4. See chapter 1, "Men and Women Are Ontologically Equal" in Phyllis Zagano, *Holy Saturday: An Argument for the Restoration of the Female Diaconate in the Catholic Church* (New York: Crossroad/Herder, 2000), 22–25.

deacons, they are equally able today to be ordained as deacons and as priests.)

To be sure, the discussion is about sacramentally ordained women deacons. The definition of *sacrament* has not changed substantially since Augustine wrote, "A sacrament is a visible sign of an invisible grace." Amid the discussions and disputes of the early twelfth century, Peter Lombard determined there were seven sacraments and wrote,

> A sacrament bears a likeness of that thing whose sign it is, "For if sacraments did not have a likeness of the things whose sacraments they are, they would properly not be called sacraments" [Augustine]. For that is properly called a sacrament which is a sign of the grace of God and a form of invisible grace, so that it bears its image and exists as its cause. Sacraments were instituted, therefore, for the sake, not only of signifying, but also of sanctifying.[5]

In the sixteenth century, the Council of Trent found there were seven and only seven sacraments, and it did not restore the diaconate as a permanent office.

The separation of priesthood and diaconate now rests in the ability and permission to perform two of those sacraments defined at Trent: Eucharist and reconciliation. Another sacrament, ordination to diaconate and priesthood, is reserved to the bishop. Reconciliation is generally understood as rendered under authority delegated by the bishop, although it can be granted by any priest in many circumstances. The determination that

5. Peter Lombard, *The Four Books of the Sentences*, IV Distinction I, 1–2, trans. Owen R. Ott, Library of Christian Classics 10:338–41, as quoted in James F. White, *Documents of Christian Worship: Descriptive and Interpretive Sources* (Louisville: Westminster John Knox Press, 1992), 122; Thomas M. Finn, "The Sacramental World in the *Sentences* of Peter Lombard," *Theological Studies* 69 (2008), 557–82.

sacramental ordination to priesthood imparted the sacred power to confect Eucharist is relatively recent in the history of the Church and appears in the documents of the Second Vatican Council, as below:

> Though they differ from one another in essence and not only in degree, the common priesthood of the faithful and the ministerial or hierarchical priesthood are nonetheless interrelated: each of them in its own special way is a participation in the one priesthood of Christ. The ministerial priest, by the sacred power he enjoys, teaches and rules the priestly people; acting in the person of Christ, he makes present the Eucharistic sacrifice, and offers it to God in the name of all the people. But the faithful, in virtue of their royal priesthood, join in the offering of the Eucharist. They likewise exercise that priesthood in receiving the sacraments, in prayer and thanksgiving, in the witness of a holy life, and by self-denial and active charity. (*Lumen gentium* 10)[6]

Looking further back in history, we find that the ministerial diaconate for the most part predates the sacerdotal priesthood. We know that in Scripture the only person with the actual job title "deacon" is Phoebe of Romans 16. Also, in Scripture, the "women likewise" of 1 Timothy 3:11 are the women deacons, required to have the same qualities of men deacons. Later, the persons chosen for ministry in Acts 6:1–6 were called forth by the apostles on recommendation of the assembly. In Acts, the four daughters of Philip the Evangelist were evangelizers themselves; they gave prophecy: "He had

---

6. Citing Col 1:15 and Rom 8:29.

four virgin daughters gifted with prophecy" (Acts 21:9, NAB). And Paul presents additional evidence: "But any woman who prays or prophesies with her head unveiled brings shame upon her head" (1 Cor 11:5, NAB). But Paul also names the women who shared his mission. In addition to Phoebe, he names Prisca and Aquila, whom he calls "fellow workers," Mary, Tryphaena, Tryphosa, and Persisi (Rom 16:1–16), and in Philippians 4:2 he speaks of Euodia and Syntyche. The words Paul uses describing these women indicate they are assistants in the works of evangelization, in the mission and ministry of the Gospel. Such is the earliest testimony of the Church; such are the words of revelation.

That they whom some call the first deacons were called forth by the apostles on nomination by the assembled Church supports the claim that the Church therefore can again present its own candidates for the diaconate. That is, there is no elimination of anyone because the Church is bound here by the choice of Jesus Christ who himself had women followers. The diaconate is the specific ministry called forth by the apostles. Even without arguing that any of the first seven (a symbolic number anyway) were female, and there are arguments to that effect, it is the assembly that put forth its candidates, candidates who were accepted by and received the laying on of hands from the apostles. That is, even if the priesthood is restricted to men because of Christ's choice of male apostles, the same restriction does not apply to the diaconate. Can the Church today accept that Jesus and the apostles chose women ministers?

In fact, the Church cannot selectively determine what it will and will not accept from history and from the actual testimony of they who nourished the earliest stirrings of Christianity in the hearts of Jesus's followers. So, to dismiss Phoebe's position, as some have, ignores the supposition that she carried Paul's letters to the Romans and denies the accepted understanding that Paul used the term "deacon" intentionally. So also, to deny that Paul's list of qualifications for deacons in 1 Timothy, that they must be "serious, not double-tongued, not indulging in much wine, not greedy for money; they must hold fast to the mystery of the faith with a clear conscience" (1 Tim 3:8), does not apply to the "women likewise" is to deny both history and grammar. The *New American Bible* translation of those ensuing words reads: "Women, similarly, should be dignified, not slandered, but temperate and faithful in everything" (1 Tim 3:11). The present footnote of the U.S. Conference of Catholic Bishops makes the positive interpretation—so often fought over by hierarchs and academics—perfectly clear. The footnote reads,

> Women: this seems to refer to women deacons but may possibly mean wives of deacons. The former is preferred because the word is used absolutely; if deacons' wives were meant a possessive "their" would be expected. Moreover, they are also introduced by the word "similarly," as in 1 Tim 3:8; this parallel suggests that they too exercised ecclesiastical functions.[7]

The keys to unlock the question are in Romans, in Timothy, in Acts, in Philippians. The evidence is in the earliest documents, frescos, liturgies, and grave markings of the Church. The evidence points clearly to women who were ordained and who served as deacons.

So, this book deals with the diaconate, not the priesthood. It deals with the ministerial diaconate, the servant diaconate, the messenger diaconate.

To be clear, the purpose of this book is to show the historical reality of ordained women deacons and to acknowledge that

---

7. See http://www.usccb.org/bible/1timothy/3.

reality. Why does the Church not reach out to half its population? Why does the Church not recognize and accept the facts of history and their implications?

The following pages review the tasks and duties of women deacons, not as mere functionaries, but as vehicles of sacramental grace. Women's roles in baptism, in catechesis, in altar service, in reconciliation and confession, and in anointing the sick show them to have been accepted and understood by the Church as sacred ministers. They were ordained deacons, and they brought the grace of sacrament to people far and wide, until they did not, until their mandate was removed and the argument that women could not image Christ gained favor in too many circles.

One theory of the etymology of the word *diakonia* is that it comes from the meaning "through the dust"; the deacon ministers, serves, and brings the message, literally, "through the dust" of the world and its afflictions. As icons of Christ, ordained women deacons served thusly.

And, after all, what do women in and of the Church do today?

1

BAPTISM

1239 The essential rite of the sacrament follows: Baptism properly speaking. It signifies and actually brings about death to sin and entry into the life of the Most Holy Trinity through configuration to the Paschal mystery of Christ. Baptism is performed in the most expressive way by triple immersion in the baptismal water. However, from ancient times it has also been able to be conferred by pouring the water three times over the candidate's head.

1240 In the Latin Church this triple infusion is accompanied by the minister's words: "N., I baptize you in the name of the Father, and of the Son, and of the Holy Spirit." In the Eastern liturgies the catechumen turns toward the East and the priest says: "The servant of God, N., is baptized in the name of the Father, and of the Son, and of the Holy Spirit." At the invocation of each person of the Most Holy Trinity, the priest immerses the candidate in the water and raises him up again.

1241 The anointing with sacred chrism, perfumed oil consecrated by the bishop, signifies the gift of the Holy Spirit to the newly baptized, who has become a Christian, that is, one "anointed" by the Holy Spirit, incorporated into Christ who is anointed priest, prophet, and king.

Catechism of the Catholic Church

ALL BAPTIZED PERSONS IMAGE CHRIST. Such is not a new or novel invention of far-out theological speculation. Baptism configures the person to Christ. All persons.

All persons are made in the image and likeness of God. All persons.

So what basis is there for any objection to the ordination of women, especially to the ordination of women as deacons?

The question is lodged in the modern discussion of priesthood. In 1976 the International Theological Commission (ITC) presented a document, *"Inter Insigniores:* On the Question of Admission of Women to the Ministerial Priesthood."[1] *Inter Insigniores* is called a "declaration," and a declaration can take three forms: (1) affirmation of an existing law; (2) authoritative presentation of a law or penalty; or (3) modification of an existing law requiring additional promulgation. So, while this document of the International Theological Commission is a "declaration," it is neither a papal nor a conciliar document; hence, its level of authority has been and is still questioned.

At most, *Inter Insigniores* renders an opinion of the Congregation for the Doctrine of the Faith, albeit one confirmed

---

1. *Inter insigniores* is translated as "among the noteworthy," referring to points in the document's argument against women priests.

and approved by Pope Paul VI. The document is dated October 15, 1976, the Feast of St. Teresa of Avila, then one of two, now one of four female doctors of the Church.[2]

The ordained diaconate of women had long died out by Teresa's time. Forced into the cloister along with the women of the early Middle Ages, the ordained diaconate for women became merely an honorific for the abbess or prioress.[3] Vestiges of the abbesses' and prioresses' juridical powers primarily attached to clerical status remained most clearly in the Cistercian Abbey of las Huelgas de Burgos in Spain, erected by Castilian King Alfonso VII and his wife Leonora in 1187. Local bishops unsuccessfully contested the abbess's jurisdictional authority, but in 1873 Pope Pius IX ended it and cancelled all other exempt monastic jurisdictions in Spain.[4] But vestiges of the abbesses' jurisdictional powers remain somewhat even today, especially in European territorial abbeys that began as royal abbeys.[5] While she no longer remits sin in confession or mixes the water and wine in the eucharistic celebration, it is the abbess or the prioress who gives permission to the person who preaches to her nuns.[6]

---

2. Teresa was declared the first female doctor of the Church in September 27, 1970, followed a few days later by Catherine of Siena, Thérèse of Lisieux in 1988, and Hildegard of Bingen in 2012.

3. Deacon-abbesses seem to have been a development of women deacons taking charge of consecrated virgins in antiquity. Teresa (Joan) White, "The Development and Eclipse of the Deacon Abbess," *Studia Patristica*, vol. 19, ed. Elizabeth A. Livingstone (Leuven: Peeters Press, 1989), 111–16.

4. *Gender in Debate from the Early Middle Ages to the Renaissance*, ed. T. S. Fenster and C. A. Lees (New York: Palgrave, 2002), 54n36, citing Josemaría Escrivá de Balaguer, *La Abadesa de las Huelgas* (Madrid: Editorial Luz, 1944).

5. An interesting study is the canon law dissertation of Josemaría Escrivá de Balaguer, *La Abadesa de las Huelgas* (Madrid: Rialp, 1944), republished as a critical edition, Maria Blanco, *La Abadesa de las Huelgas*, vol. 5, Complete Works of Saint Josemaría Escrivá de Balaguer (Madrid: Rialp, 2016).

6. Canon 765. Preaching to religious in their churches or oratories requires the permission of the superior competent according to the norms of the constitutions.

WOMEN: ICONS OF CHRIST

For hundreds of years, outside the abbey or monastery, women continued to serve in diaconal roles, even when not ordained to such service. During the fourteenth century, even as a young woman Catherine of Siena joined the Mantellate, the Dominican third order comprised of widows of the area who found their ministerial places with good works in their city. They went about plague-ravaged Siena bringing food to the poor, ministering to ill women, and burying the dead.

The vocation of women to serve people in need—and especially to serve women and children and vulnerable persons in need—has perdured over the centuries. Sisters of Saint Joseph around the world celebrate their founder's day coincidentally enough on the Feast of Teresa of Avila, recalling the date six women gathered in Le Puy, France, to serve their "dear neighbors" as apostolic religious. These first Sisters of St. Joseph, gathered by Jesuit Jean Pierre Médaille on October 15, 1650, whose numbers have grown exponentially over the centuries, lived in small groups and, like Catherine and the Mantellates, ministered outside the cloister. Their work is and has been quite varied. They are not deacons, nor need they be. Their ministries are varied and their reasons for joining their institutes come first from the desire for consecrated life. Even so, the animating spirit of diaconal service is clear throughout their histories to the present.

Women deacons as such disappeared in the West in the late Middle Ages. So, by the seventeenth century, as the Sisters of Saint Joseph and other institutes of apostolic women religious were founded, there were no Western women deacons. Neither were there Western women deacons in the twentieth century, when *Inter Insigniores* was published. The diaconate of women remained and remains in pockets of the East, where the older tradition has not been abandoned or has been recovered.[7] What is important about *Inter Insigniores* is that, while it states that women cannot image Christ, it pointedly leaves aside the question of women ordained as deacons. Such has been the modern history of the question of women deacons, even as it continues to be mixed up with the question of women priests and, tangentially, with questions about contemporary apostolic religious life for women.

As far as ordination is concerned, the discussions of the latter half of the twentieth century, as they have moved into the twenty-first century, increasingly point to what is called the unicity of orders in addition to the so-called iconic argument that states women cannot image Christ. There are three distinct grades to the sacrament of order: deacon, priest, and bishop. However, the concept of the "unicity of orders" carries with it the implication that a person capable of receiving the sacrament of order in one grade is, or at least theoretically should be, able to receive the sacrament of order in any of the others. The concept adheres to a staged understanding of orders: one is first ordained a deacon, then a priest, then a bishop. Such is the now-discarded program of the *cursus honorum*, the progression of orders as it developed and eventually solidified in the Middle Ages. Anyone ordained as deacon would be on his way to priesthood. In fact, only men could enter the stages toward priestly ordination: tonsure, porter, lector, exorcist, acolyte, sub-deacon, deacon, priest. Tonsure signified the clerical status of the candidate, who was first ordained (typically within the sacristy) to the minor orders

---

7. Phyllis Zagano, "Catholic Women's Ordination: The Ecumenical Implications of Women Deacons in the Armenian Apostolic Church, the Orthodox Church of Greece, and Union of Utrecht Old Catholic Churches," *Journal of Ecumenical Studies* 43, no. 1 (Winter 2008): 124-37. In 2016, the Patriarchate of Alexandria voted to restore the order of women deacons, several of whom were ceremonially appointed in February 2017. There remains conjecture as to the nature of the liturgy.

of porter, lector, exorcist, and acolyte before being ordained to the major orders of sub-deacon, deacon, and priest.

The codification of the *cursus honorum* caused the diaconate to essentially disappear as a separate order of ministry; it became instead merely a step on the way to priesthood. In different eras, individuals were ordained and remained deacons for only a few hours—or a day or a few months—before being ordained as priests. (Today, such is the case in some territories, where seminarians are ordained deacons "in house" and remain deacons for only a few months.) What is important to recognize here is that there were—and still are—separate ordinations for deacon and priest. Further, as of 2017, there were some 47,000 men (predominantly married men) who serve in the diaconate as a permanent vocation throughout the world.[8]

The early Church did not see ministry only in progressive stages—deacon, priest, bishop. In fact, the first Church ministries were episcopal and diaconal, the overseers and the helpers; these two mentioned in Scripture mark the clear division between what came to be more formally understood as episcopal ministry and what came to be more formally understood as diaconal ministry. Broadly speaking, if we focus on the institution of the Eucharist at the Last Supper, the work of the apostles was episcopal and pastoral in that they oversaw the regulation of the nascent Christian community, its ceremonies of initiation, and the Liturgy of the Eucharist. Their helpers, the "servants in the dust," whom we can look to as the first diaconal ministers, were just that: helpers.

Although the earliest women "helpers," the first to perform diaconal ministry, were not necessarily regulators of the Christian community, increasingly they managed the church's finances and stores. They were not necessarily the leaders of

---

8. *Annuarium Statisticum Ecclesiae* 2017.

ceremonies of initiation, although they certainly assisted in the baptisms by immersion common at the time, anointing women *baptizandae*.[9] They were not necessarily the preachers of the Word at celebrations of the Eucharist, although they clearly catechized women and children. They were not necessarily authoritative judges, but they did provide testimony in cases of spousal abuse. They were not necessarily ministering to all persons, but they did ritually anoint, give spiritual direction, and even remit the sins of other women in confession. They were not necessarily celebrants of the Liturgy of the Eucharist, although as rituals developed, at times they were the ministers of the cup and assisted in other ways during the liturgy.

Every place and every era did not see identical developments, but early women deacons were ministers of the Word, of the liturgy, and of charity in their teaching, in their ceremonial functions, and in their charitable and administrative tasks. They were chosen by the ecclesial leadership and, as structures and rituals developed, they were ordained to these duties with the laying on of hands. They continued to be so chosen, and to be so ordained, up until the twelfth century in the West and, apparently, to the present in portions of the East.

---

9. They "administer the sacrament of baptism of women because it is not proper for the priest to see the nudity of women. Therefore, the deaconess must anoint the women and baptize them with water. The priest must only put his hand through the window or behind the curtain and sign the candidates; deaconesses perform the baptism and the anointing." From the *Liber Patrum*, composed between the twelfth and fourteenth centuries. Pietro Sorci, "The Diaconate and Other Liturgical Ministries of Women," in *Women Deacons? Essays with Answers*, ed. Phyllis Zagano (Collegeville, MN: Liturgical Press, 2016), 69–70; "Diaconato e altri ministeri liturgici della donna," in *La Donna nel pensiero Cristiano antico*, ed. Umberto Mattioli (Genova: Marietti Editori, 1992), 331–64.

DEVELOPMENT OF
THE HIERARCHY

The early Church as a secular organization (that is, distinct from a monastery or religious order) developed its hierarchical structure along the pyramidal organizational structure of the Roman army. Yet the Church's territorial-hierarchical structure allowed a simple means by which new Christian assemblies could be cared for within certain territories overseen by the persons who came to be called bishops (*episcopi*) and who were eventually aided by the development of a separate group of individuals (*presbyters*), today called priests. Early on, the overseers quite formally had helpers in ministry, *diakoni*, or deacons, male and female.

The Christian message attracted many new followers, from within and without the Jewish community. As the early Church opened its arms to more and more people, the Jewish Christians found themselves distinctive, because they had undergone circumcision. Non-Jewish converts posed a problem: Did they need to receive circumcision before being baptized Christian? We can note in Scripture one extremely important point: No one was talking directly about women joining the community, even as there is ample scriptural evidence that women did belong and in fact were leaders in many Christian communities.

Certainly, the question of circumcision did not arise regarding women converts, although I did once hear a seminary professor in class equate male circumcision with baptism and speaking of "female circumcision"—more generally known as female genital mutilation—as the separate but equal ritual for women. Such speaks more of ignorance than of history. The fact of the matter is there is no such discussion about women who converted from Judaism to Christianity. One can assume the women followed their husbands or other family

8

groupings, or that their husbands or other family groupings followed them. In any event, we know there were women followers of Jesus and that there were women among the earliest Christians. So, too, were there women ministers among the earliest Christians who, as noted earlier, are attested to by literary, epigraphical, and artistic evidence. They were baptized and they assisted in the baptisms of others.

These earliest women ministers were called deacons, not deaconesses, until language changed in many places to accommodate gender. Their place at the baptismal pool with women neophytes is well documented and well known. But what earned them that right? How did some women, and not others, earn a place at and participation in the conferral of the sacrament of baptism?

To understand the fact that the early Church included women ministers in the performance of sacred tasks, we must look at the various ceremonies by which bishops (no doubt on recommendation from the ecclesial community) ordained them to the ministry that we know today as the diaconate. But before the diaconate became known as an ordained ministry, women were already living it. We cannot forget that women supported and accompanied Jesus in his mission, even to the cross, where the men had essentially abandoned him. It was a woman who anointed Jesus in preparation for his passion. And it was women who were first at the tomb, there to anoint his body.[10] Truly, women, soon known as women deacons, had an integral role in the building up of the early Church.

---

10. Several women are attested to in Scripture as being part of Jesus's mission. Mary Magdalene, Joanna, and Susanna are mentioned in Luke 8:1-3; 23:49, 55; 24:10; and Matthew and Mark also note women accompanying Jesus (Matt 27:55-56; Mark 15:40-41). Matthew and Mark state that many women were at the crucifixion in addition to Mary Magdalene and Mary, the mother of Jesus. Women went to the tomb to anoint the body of Jesus, and it was Mary Magdalene to whom the Risen Lord first appeared (Matt 28:1-10; Mark 16:1; Luke 24; John 20:1-18).

Scripture attests to women among the ministerial helpers to the earliest overseers, the *episcopoi* we now call bishops. These were the women deacons who would catechize and eventually assist in the baptisms of new Christian women. Following Phoebe, following the women noted in Timothy, following (as some argue) the woman among the first seven chosen by the apostles as recorded in Acts, there are women who were selected and ordained to their service within the ancient churches of Christianity.

PHOEBE OF ROMANS 16:1

We trace the beginnings to Phoebe. Paul in his greetings to the Romans makes Phoebe's status quite clear: "I commend to you our sister Phoebe, a deacon of the church at Cenchreae" (Rom 16:1).

While some contemporary commentators begin their denials of women as deacons with Paul's calling Phoebe "deacon"—even incorrectly translating Scripture to call her a deaconess—a majority of the earliest Christian commentators accept her status, including Origen, John Chrysostom, and Theodoret of Cyrrhus. There was one major naysayer: a commentator on Paul's letters who was quite influential in the Middle Ages, later proved not to be Ambrose, the great bishop of Milan, even though the medievalists so identified him. He came to be called Ambrosiaster, or pseudo-Ambrose.

But among those who found Phoebe the true herald of the diaconate was Origen, an early Greek Christian theologian born toward the end of the second century and who lived until 253 or 254. Some of Origen's theological writings became controversial, but his historical understandings of Scripture are not widely challenged. Origen's extensive body of work falls into three categories: his summaries of difficult passages of Scripture, his homilies, and his commentaries on Scripture.

Commenting on Romans 16:1—2, the passage in which Paul refers to Phoebe as a deacon, Origen says quite plainly that the early Church, as attested to by this passage, included women appointed to the Church's ministry:

> This passage teaches by apostolic authority that women are appointed (*constitui*) in the ministry of the church (*in ministerio ecclesiae*), in which office Phoebe was placed at the church that is in Cenchreae....And therefore this passage teaches two things equally and is to be interpreted, as we have said, to mean that women are to be considered ministers (*haberi...feminas ministras*) in the church, and that such [women] ought to be received into the ministry (*tales debere assumi in ministerium*) who have assisted many.[11]

Unfortunately, this passage exists only in Latin, not in its original Greek, which may account for some apparent double meanings. While Origen does not explicitly call the women "deacons," there are dual meanings of the words *feminas ministras*: women deacons or women ministers. Equally, there are differing ways of interpreting Origen's meaning as to whether women are to be accepted into a generalized or more specific "ministry" as ministers or as deacons: *tales debere assumi in ministerium*. What is quite clear is that Origen

---

11. Kevin Madigan and Carolyn Osiek, *Ordained Women in the Early Church: A Documentary History* (Baltimore and London: John's Hopkins University Press, 2005), 14; from *Monumenta de viduis diaconissis virginibusque tractantia*, Florilegium Patristicum 42, ed. Josephine Mayer (Bonn: Peter Hanstein, 1938), 8-9.

considers these women as part and parcel of the nascent ministering but hierarchical Church.

Origen's observations are followed by those of the great preacher John Chrysostom (ca. 347–407), a deacon and later priest of the Greek city of Antioch, located within present-day Turkey, who became bishop of Constantinople in 398. Commenting on Paul's calling Phoebe a deacon, Chrysostom quite plainly accepts her status. Given that he is known to have had many friends among the ministering church in Constantinople, where he was rather politically incorrect, we can assume with other scholars that he was at the very least equating Phoebe with the contemporary deaconesses Olympias, Pentadia, and Procla, who defended Chrysostom but did not forestall his being sent into exile.[12] In fact, prior to his exile, Chrysostom ordained three women relatives of Olympias—Palladia, Elisanthia, and Martyria—to diaconal service.[13]

Not long after Chrysostom affirmed Phoebe as deacon, another native of Antioch, Theodoret of Cyrrhus (ca. 393–460), affirmed her status. Theodoret was involved in the Nestorian controversy[14] and active at the Council of Chalcedon (451), the fifteenth canon of which set the age of ordination of women deacons at forty-two and also proscribed their marriage after ordination.[15] The canon is widely understood as affirming

---

12. Madigan and Osiek, *Women in the Early Church*, 14-15, citing *PG* 60:663-64, J. Bousquet, "Vie d'Olympias la deaconess," *Revue de l'Orient chrétien*, Deuxième Série, Tome I (XI) (1906): 225-50.

13. Philip F. Esler, *The Early Christian World* (Abingdon-on-Thames: Routledge Worlds, 2000, 2004), 1132-33.

14. Denial of the hypostatic union, rather presenting an argument that the human Jesus put on divine nature proposed by Nestorius, a fifth-century bishop of Constantinople, who also refused to call Mary the mother of God.

15. In classical Greece and Rome, the average life expectancy was fewer than thirty years. In Rome, persons who survived to age twenty could be expected to live to fifty. Bruce Frier, "Demographics," in *The Cambridge Ancient History, Vol. 11: The High Empire, A.D. 70-192* (Cambridge: Cambridge University Press, 2000), 788-89. In Greece the outside prediction would be forty-one years. J.

both the true ordination of women deacons and the fact that they were part of the clergy, as the practice of forbidding marriage (or remarriage) after entering the clerical state was by this time well-established. Theodoret interprets Romans 16 in this way: "Such was the significance of the church at Cenchreae that it had a female deacon, honorable and well-known."[16]

Nevertheless, not all commentators—ancient or modern—accept Phoebe as deacon. Some prefer the Latin word *ministra* to mean only helper, even as it is used by others to mean, as well as female deacon or deaconess. One example of this is in the writings of Ambrosiaster mentioned earlier, who wrote what is apparently the oldest Latin commentary on the Letters of St. Paul, dated in the fourth century, but which depended on Latin, not Greek, scriptures for its exegesis.[17] Hence Ambrosiaster could have uncritically picked up the word *ministra* and called Phoebe "helper" rather than "minister." Such, of course, demotes her from her privileged position as patron and deacon and presages the type of misogynistic and androcentric rewriting of Scripture and of history the Church suffers to this day.

An interesting point about Ambrosiaster—aside from the fact that his name means "pseudo-Ambrose"—is that no one knows quite who he was. The famous Dutch Christian humanist Erasmus proved in the sixteenth century that Ambrosiaster was not Ambrose of Milan, the doctor of the Church who lived in the late fourth century, well after the documents for many centuries falsely attributed to him were written. Hence the negative and somewhat dismissive attitude Ambrosiaster evidenced toward women was not that of Ambrose, although it carried the bishop

---

Lawrence Angel, "The Bases of Paleodemography," *American Journal of Physical Anthropology* 30, no. 3 (May 1969): 427–37.

16. Madigan and Osiek, *Women in the Early Church*, 16, citing *PG* 82.809.

17. Madigan and Osiek, *Women in the Early Church*, 17–18, discuss Ambrosiaster; *CSEL* 83 (1966): 476–77.

and saint's gravitas for many centuries. Also interesting is that Ambrosiaster's attitude toward Phoebe as deacon is among the first, if not the first, denial of the fact that women were even called deacons. Ambrosiaster's downplaying of Phoebe's role, quite plainly presented by Paul as deacon of the Church at Cenchreae, prepares the way for others determined to keep women from the sanctuary and the sacred.

THE WOMEN OF 1 TIMOTHY 3:11

Paul's letters include another, more general reference to women who served the early Church in the diaconate. In 1 Timothy 3:11, Paul specifically refers to "women." In the *New American Bible* translation, the interesting sentence appears just after Paul lists the various qualifications for deacons, who "must be serious, not double-tongued, not indulging in much wine, not greedy for money; they must hold fast to the mystery of the faith with a clear conscience" (1 Tim 3:8–9). The famous and often contested sentence that appears soon after reads in this translation, accepted by the U.S. Conference of Catholic Bishops: "Women likewise must be serious, not slanderers, but temperate, faithful in all things." Other translations speak of the "women, similarly." Recall the U.S. Conference of Catholic Bishops' footnote for that very interesting sentence in 1 Timothy—"This seems to refer to women deacons"—and that the main opponent to this interpretation is Abrosiaster, the pseudo-Ambrose of whom nothing is known.

The context of the sentence, which obviously lists ministerial qualifications, solidifies the interpretation that women ministered in the diaconate and Paul accepted and ratified their ministry.

John Chrysostom, Clement of Alexandria, Theodoret of

Cyrrhus, Theodore of Mopsuestia, and Pelagius each affirmed that the passage in 1 Timothy referred to women deacons.

John Chrysostom directly addresses any objections: "Some say that he [Paul] is writing about women in general.... But, rather he is speaking of those women who hold the rank of deacon."[18] Of course John's churches in Antioch and Constantinople had women ordained to the diaconate, so he would be interpreting both from custom and from his own understanding of the text.

Clement of Alexandria clearly believed women deacons were, in fact, deacons. His comment on their contemporary value in his era includes one pertinent fact: he referred to the women deacons simply as διάκονοι γυναῖκες (deacon women), whose ministry allowed the Gospel to be brought to women.[19]

Theodoret of Cyrrhus, like John a supporter of the interpretation of Romans 16:1 that understands Phoebe as deacon, establishes the parallel instructions of 1 Timothy to the men and the women. Theodoret writes, "What he [Paul] directed for the men he did similarly for the women." By pointing out the parallelism of the commands, Theodoret also establishes a parallelism of duties. Whereas men deacons were to be serious, so also should be the women; whereas men deacons should not be, in Theodoret's words, "two-faced," the women should not "talk irresponsibly"; and where men deacons ought not drink too much wine, so "the women should be temperate."[20]

Finally, Theodore of Mopsuestia's commentary on the passage from 1 Timothy says outright that Paul does not mean it is fitting for deacons to have wives; rather, "it is fitting for

18. Madigan and Osiek, *Women in the Early Church*, 19, citing *PG* 62.553; Mayer, *Monumenta*, 18.

19. John N. Collins, "Διάκον- and Deacons in Clement of Alexandria," in *Deacons and Diakonia in Early Christianity*, ed. Koet/Murphy/Ryökäs (Tübingen: Mohr Siebeck), citing *Stromata* 3.6.53.

20. Madigan and Osiek, *Women in the Early Church*, 19, citing *PG* 82.809.

women to be established to perform duties similar to those of deacons." Theodoret lists other attributes, especially the ability to be discreet and keep confidences, qualities clearly necessary to ministry.[21]

The three early exegetes listed above are joined by Pelagius, a British- (some say Irish-) born exegete who, around the year 410, equates the women in 1 Timothy with "those who still today in the East are called deaconesses."[22]

Still, only Ambrosiaster argues that the women were not "deacons," and he uses the passage as his starting point to argue that women cannot or at least ought not to be ordained. In a fascinating passage, Ambrosiaster accepts the Pauline prohibition against women speaking in the assembly and argues that despite the holiness of the women who ministered with the apostles, they were not chosen for ministry due to their gender.[23] It is difficult to accept Ambrosiaster's commentary here or elsewhere because, despite its erudition, it is so obviously biased against women and so peppered with misogyny. What mitigates most against Ambrosiaster is not so much his view as his somewhat acidic and condescending tone, perhaps directed more at what he found as abuses of his own fourth century than presenting an elucidation of Scripture.

ACTS OF THE APOSTLES 6:1-6

While some attach the beginnings of diaconal ministry to Jesus's example of washing the feet of the apostles at the Last Supper, this act, often considered his final example of direct ministry to others, can also be understood as either an addi-

---

21. Madigan and Osiek, *Women in the Early Church*, 19–20, citing Sweete, *In Epistolas*, 2.128.

22. Madigan and Osiek, *Women in the Early Church*, 20–21, citing *PL* 30.880.

23. Madigan and Osiek, *Women in the Early Church*, 20, citing Ambrosiaster, *Commentarius in Epistulas Paulinas*, CSEL 81 (1969): 267–68.

tional or an included charge to the service the apostles were to render in and to the nascent *ecclesia*, the early Church. In any event, there is clear indication of the development and formalization of ministries in the Church with the testimony of Acts 6:1–6:

> Now during those days, when the disciples were increasing in number, the Hellenists complained against the Hebrews because their widows were being neglected in the daily distribution of food. And the twelve called together the whole community of the disciples and said, "It is not right that we should neglect the word of God in order to wait on tables. Therefore, friends, select from among yourselves seven men of good standing, full of the Spirit and of wisdom, whom we may appoint to this task, while we, for our part, will devote ourselves to prayer and to serving the word. What they said pleased the whole community, and they chose Stephen, a man full of faith and the Holy Spirit, together with Philip, Prochorus, Nicanor, Timon, Parmenas, and Nicolaus, a proselyte of Antioch. They had these men stand before the apostles, who prayed and laid their hands on them.

There are several important points here. First, we see the growing numbers of disciples, they who must minister and who must be ministered to; second, we note it is the assembly that puts forth the candidates for the implied diaconal service the apostles requested; third, it is the apostles who accepted and laid hands on these seven on behalf of the Church; and, finally, while the Scripture passage names seven men (the Latin text reads: *vivorum*), it more probably describes an ideal rather than an exact historical situation.

So, even if women are not named in this instance, the number of disciples—including women disciples–was growing. Also, they who were to serve were both put forth by the assembly, and they received the laying on of hands from the apostles. That is, the establishment of the diaconate as a ministry that eventually became solidified as part of the hierarchy was an action of the Church ratified by the Church.

The fact that the diaconate was a creation of the Church cannot be forgotten. When speaking in Philadelphia to bishops on his 2015 trip to the United States, Pope Francis made this very point:

> In the early days of the Church, the Hellenists complained that their widows and orphans were not being well cared for. The apostles, of course, weren't able to handle this themselves, so they got together and came up with deacons. The Holy Spirit inspired them to create deacons and when Peter announced the decision, he explained: "We are going to choose seven men to take care of this; for our part, we have two responsibilities: prayer and preaching."[24]

The apostles essentially "invented" the diaconate. That is, the diaconate is connected to the ministry of the apostles but disconnected from Jesus's choice of apostles and clearly open to modification and change. Women were chosen, and later ordained, as deacons from the earliest days of the Church, but one need not agree with that fact because history alone is not dispositive. That is, whether one does or does not accept that women were chosen and eventually sacramentally ordained

---

24. Meeting with bishops taking part in the World Meeting of Families, Address of the Holy Father, September 27, 2015, http://w2.vatican.va/content/francesco/en/speeches/2015/september/documents/papa-francesco_20150927_usa-vescovi-festa-famiglie.html.

to the diaconate, the diaconate's mutability is rooted in the fact that it is a creation of the Church.

This is not to suggest that women were not sacramentally ordained deacons or that women did not serve in true diaconal ministry. The baptism of women presents the prime example given on both sides of the discussion. We can recall here that the early Church practiced full or partial immersion baptism and that, as the ministry of deacons developed, the ministry of women deacons included assisting the bishop in its administration. Hence, aside from genuine evidence that women were formally included in the diaconal ministry, we must recall that their inclusion in this ministry was necessary in the ancient world, where modesty and propriety required women to assist other women in baptismal ceremonies, which included partial or complete lack of clothing and anointing of the body, followed by catechetical instructions of various durations.[25]

Even so, the diaconate—at least as attested to in its inception in Scripture—resulted from the call of the apostles to the community to provide individuals to assist with the Church's charity. Before Pope Francis reminded the assembled bishops in Philadelphia of the ecclesial beginnings of the diaconate, Pope Benedict XVI spoke of the establishment of the diaconate as a ministry of the Church. In his first encyclical, *Deus caritas est*, Benedict points out that the crucial task of the diaconate is ministry to the community. He speaks of the "radical form of material communion" among the members of the early Christian community that could not be sustained or preserved because of the growing numbers of followers of Christ. But, he adds, "Its essential core remained: Within the community

---

25. The ancient world universally separated men from women, and women attended to other women in specifically female rituals. Jewish purification rites come to mind, as well as various Greek, Roman, and Egyptian rituals.

of believers there can never be room for a poverty that denies anyone what is needed for a dignified life" (para. 20).[26]

Benedict here refers directly to the diaconal ministry of charity, a ministry he later connects explicitly and directly with the Word and with the liturgy, pointing out that it is Christian charity, not secular social service, that deacons are called to. Neither in this section nor elsewhere in the encyclical does he address the baptism or catechesis of neophytes, perhaps because female baptism and catechesis of women and the young were historically the charge of women deacons, and Benedict does not connect the formal ministry of the diaconate with women.

As for the initiation of the diaconate, and the "fundamental principle" that "there can never be room for a poverty that denies anyone what is needed for a dignified life," Benedict writes,

> 21. A decisive step in the difficult ways for putting this fundamental ecclesial principle into practice is illustrated in the choice of the seven, which marked the origin of the diaconal office (cf. Acts 6:5–6). In the early Church, in fact, with regard to the daily distribution to widows, a disparity had arisen between Hebrew speakers and Greek speakers. The Apostles, who had been entrusted primarily with "prayer" (the Eucharist and the liturgy) and the "ministry of the word" felt over-burdened by "serving tables," so they decided to reserve to themselves the principal duty and to designate for the other task, also necessary in the Church, a group of seven persons. Nor was this group to carry out a purely mechanical

---

26. Benedict XVI, Encyclical Letter *Deus caritas est* (December 25, 2005), http://www.vatican.va/holy_father/benedict_xvi/encyclicals/documents/hf_ben -xvi_enc_20051225_deus-caritas-est_en.html (accessed October 21, 2014).

work of distribution: they were to be men "full of the Spirit and of wisdom" (cf. Acts 6:1–6). In other words, the social service which they were meant to provide was absolutely concrete, yet at the same time it was also a spiritual service; theirs was a truly spiritual office which carried out an essential responsibility of the Church, namely a well-ordered love of neighbor. With the formation of this group of seven, "*diaconia*"—the ministry of charity exercised in a communitarian, orderly way—became part of the fundamental structure of the Church. (*Deus caritas est* 21)

Benedict's vision of Church here and elsewhere in his encyclical demonstrates the principles his successor, Francis, articulated early on and continually during his own papacy. What is so interesting in Benedict's encyclical, which comments copiously on the diaconate, is that while he clearly situates the beginnings of the diaconate in Acts, and he speaks to the calling of "a group of seven persons" (not seven men), he ignores the scriptural documentation of women in diaconal roles, including Phoebe, again the only person in Scripture with the job title "deacon."[27]

Further, while in the paragraph immediately following the one quoted above Benedict writes of the Church's deep involvement with charity, he overlooks any history of women deacons, including and especially they who were ordained by their bishops to the diaconate. He lists charity, so often completely within the purview of women or nearly so, as one of

---

27. Benedict's androcentric projection onto the three ministries leaves no room for diaconate of men and women, since he cannot uncouple the diaconal ministry from those of presbyter and bishop. See Joseph Ratzinger, *Called to Communion: Understanding the Church Today*, trans Adrian Walker (San Francisco: Ignatius Press, 1991).

the Church's "essential activities" but finds no connection between charity and the ministries performed by women as the Church grew. Benedict writes,

> 22. As the years went by and the Church spread further afield, the exercise of charity became established as one of her essential activities, along with the administration of the sacraments and the proclamation of the word: love for widows and orphans, prisoners, and the sick and needy of every kind, is as essential to her as the ministry of the sacraments and preaching of the Gospel. The Church cannot neglect the service of charity any more than she can neglect the sacraments and the word. (*Deus caritas est* 22)

Benedict cites Justin Martyr († c. 155), Tertullian († after 220), and Ignatius of Antioch († c. 117) as attesting to the Church's rendering of charity as its distinctive function. He discusses the history of the diaconate, omitting the women who served in it. In fact, throughout the entire encyclical he names but four women: Louise de Marillac (1591–1660), Teresa of Calcutta (1910–97), Mary, the mother of Jesus, and Elizabeth, Mary's cousin.[28]

One can make ample argument that Louise de Marillac, founder of the Sisters of Charity (with St. Vincent de Paul), and Mother Teresa, who founded the Missionaries of Charity, were the unordained women deacons of the Renaissance and of modernity. In fact, the diminishment of the diaconate and its reduction to ceremonial functions during the Middle Ages left the Church bereft of diaconal ministry. Eventually, that need was filled by women and men who founded apostolic religious

---

28. For a more complete evaluation of Benedict's view of the diaconate, see Phyllis Zagano, "The Revisionist History of Benedict XVI," *Harvard Divinity Bulletin* 34, no. 2 (Spring 2006): 72-77.

institutes specifically for the charitable and educational needs of the people of God.

While convents did exist, there was movement in Europe toward the founding of what came to be called apostolic religious life for both men and for women in the sixteenth and seventeenth centuries. For example, in 1633, Louise de Marillac initiated a life form whereby women were not bound to their convents with enclosure. They did not profess the solemn vows of monastic and contemplative orders but rather made annual simple vows so they might be free of cloister to serve the poor. Similarly, Mother Teresa's Missionaries of Charity, following the great trajectory of modern apostolic religious life, are not wholly cloistered where their ministry is to the poor. Between the sixteenth and twentieth centuries women founded hundreds of institutes to perform diaconal works.

But there is a great gap in Benedict's recital of the development of the diaconate within the growing charge of charity for all members of the Church. Yes, Louise and Teresa provided diaconal service. In Louise's era, the diaconate had effectively died out. In Mother Teresa's time, a portion of the diaconate was being renewed. The great disconnect, even today, is between the charitable and catechetical work of women and the ordained diaconate.

We know women have entered diaconal work throughout history, up to modern times. Women continued diaconal work, but once the diaconate as a functioning ministry died out, and those women deacons who remained were enclosed in cloister, it was left for laywomen to take up the diaconal ministries of the Church. Such is the case today.

Yet if the women ordained to ministry were not deacons, what were they? Archeological evidence from the East and from the West calls them deacons—or deaconesses—or by the abbreviations "*diac*" or "*diak*." The epigraphical evidence, existing tombstone inscriptions, clearly place women deacons in Palestine, in Jerusalem, at the Mount of Olives from the fourth to the seventh centuries.[29] There is a seventh-century inscription from Moab (Jordan) of the "*dk* Maria."[30]

There are, according to Ute Eisen of Goethe University (Frankfurt), "countless" inscriptions for women deacons in Asia Minor: for Timothea in Cilicia (southeastern coast of Turkey), for Maria in Cappadocia (east central Turkey), for Basilissa in Lycaonia (central Turkey), for Paula and others in Phrygia (western Turkey), for Eugenia in Bithynia (northwest Turkey).[31]

There are inscriptions from Greece: for the deacon Agalliasis in Cyclades (Greek islands southeast of the mainland), for the deacon Agrippa in Patras in Achaia (northwestern Greece), for Anathanasia in Delphi (southwestern Greece).[32]

There are inscriptions from Macedonia: for the "*diak*" Theoprep(e)ia in Bonitsa, for the "*diak*" Posidonia and the deacon Agathe in Philippi, for the deacon Agathokleia and the deacon Theodosia in Edessa.[33]

There are more inscriptions in the West: in Rome, for "*diac*" Anna (sixth century); in Dalmatia (Croatia, eastern cost of the Adriatic Sea), for "*diac*" Ausonia (sixth century); in Gaul (France), for *diaconissa* Theodora (d. 539).[34]

Recalling the combined negative forces against surviving

---

29. Ute E. Eisen, *Women Officeholders in Early Christianity: Epigraphical and Literary Studies*, trans. Linda Maloney (Collegeville, MN: Liturgical Press, 2000), 158–60.

30. Eisen, *Women Officeholders*, 160–61.

31. Eisen, *Women Officeholders*, 164–74.

32. Eisen, *Women Officeholders*, 174–77.

33. Eisen, *Women Officeholders*, 178–82.

34. Eisen, *Women Officeholders*, 182–85. For Anna, Eisen cites *ICUR* n.s. II 4788 (G.B. de Rossi, completed and edited by Angelus Silvagni et al., *Inscriptions christianae Urbis Romae septimo saeculo antiquiores*, new series, 11 vols. [Rome: Ex Officina Libraria Doct. Befani, 1922–1985]). Kaufmann, *Handbuch der altrchristlichen Epigraphik*, 294, considers it much more recent than 539. For Ausonia, Eisen notes that Martimort dates this as sixth century because he asserts there were not deaconesses in the West before then. Eisen notes Theodora in Kaufmann, *Handbuch der altrchristlichen Epigraphik*, 294.

inscriptions with the efforts of local synods and councils in the fifth and sixth centuries to legislate against women deacons, Church historian Kevin Madigan (Harvard) and New Testament and early Christianity scholar Carolyn Osiek (emerita, Brite Divinity School) find that women deacons were more present in the West than the numbers of inscriptions and even literary references would indicate. They add Accepta in Africa Proconsularis (near Carthage, in present-day Tunisia) to Eisen's list.[35] It is important to note that Eisen's work was published first in German in 1996, and Madigan and Osiek's in 2005, and, although what they collectively present is enough to demonstrate the existence and acceptance of women deacons outside monasteries, the ensuing years have brought forth even more epigraphical findings up to and including the sixth century and after.[36]

In fact, it is in the sixth century that Caesarius, bishop of Arles in Gaul (France), creates a monastery for his sister, whom he ordains deacon. Caesarius writes for her and her sisters the work popularly known as a *Rule for Nuns*, even as its proper title is *Regula virginium* (Rule for Virgins), and marks perhaps decisively the delineation between women deacons who were part of the community—as wives, widows, and virgins—and enclosed nuns, who might be widows or virgins. It further marks the end, or at least the beginnings of the end, of women deacons as part of the public ministering Church. Finally, it supports the historical understanding that women deacons or at least one woman deacon took charge of consecrated virgins, often after their parents died, and that such was the precursor of abbess-deacons.[37]

---

35. Madigan and Osiek, *Women in the Early Church*, 143, 209.

36. See, for example, Christine Schenck, *Crispina and Her Sisters: Women and Authority in Early Christianity* (Minneapolis, MN: Fortress Press, 2017).

37. Teresa Joan White, "The Development and Eclipse of the Deacon Abbess," *Studia Patristica*, vol. 19, ed. Elizabeth A. Livingstone (Leuven: Peeters Press, 1989), 111–16. Caesarius's work is dated 512.

WOMEN: ICONS OF CHRIST

It is in the sixth century that Radegund (or Radegunda, ca. 520–87) was ordained by Bishop Médard de Noyon. Born in Erfut (in Germany), Radegund—now St. Radegund—was a Thuringian princess and Frankish queen, and founder of the Abbey of the Holy Cross at Poitiers in present-day France. Following a battle victory in 531, Clotaire I chose young Radegund as his sixth wife; he married her in 540 when she was twenty. Eventually, Radegund fled Clotaire's castle and begged Bishop Médard to ordain her to the diaconate, which he did in 560, and she founded her abbey at Poitiers. The women who lived around her followed Caesarius's *Rule*, learned to read and write, studied Scripture, did needlework, and in today's terms lived a contemplative monastic life. Radegund was a deacon-abbess. While many churches in England, France, and Austria are named for Radegund, and she is the patron of Jesus College, Cambridge, what is notable about her story is that, first, she was consecrated as deacon: "He [Médard] laid his hand on her and consecrated (*consecravit*) her a deacon (*diaconam*)."[38]

By the sixth century, the women who were consecrated, blessed, or ordained as deacons (the terms were used interchangeably) engaged in ministries quite different from those in the early Church where, we must recall, among their principal duties was assisting at the baptisms of women and the catechesis of them and of children, in addition to care of the sick. The movement away from immersion baptism obviated the need for this task of women deacons. Even so, the need for catechesis of women and children remained.

---

38. Madigan and Osiek, *Women in the Early Church*, 143, citing *Venanti Honori Clementiani Fortunati presbyteri italici Opera pedestria*, ed. Bruno Krusch, MGH Antiquissimi (Berlin: Weidemanns, 1885), 4.2, 41.

2

CATECHESIS & CATECHISMS

Women should be silent in the churches. For they are not permitted to speak, but should be subordinate, as the law also says. If there is anything they desire to know, let them ask their husbands at home. For it is shameful for a woman to speak in church.

1 Corinthians 14:34-35[1]

T HIS WELL-KNOWN PASSAGE is attributed to St. Paul, although its authorship is disputed.[2] The author, if indeed it was Paul, would likely be writing from Ephesus on the west coast of modern Turkey, approximately 240 miles

---

1. Some translations have it "disgraceful" for a woman to speak in church.

2. Significant scholarship claims this passage was not written by Paul, or at least was inserted in the manuscript to suit the worldview of Western editors. See, for example, David W. Odell-Scott, "Editorial Dilemma: The Interpolation of 1 Cor 14:34-35 in the Western Manuscripts of D, G and 88," *Biblical Theology Bulletin* 30, no. 2 (Summer 2000): 68-74; and Philip B. Payne, "Ms 88 as Evidence for a Text without 1 Cor 14:34-35," *New Testament Studies* 44, no. 1 (January 1998): 152-58.

from the obstreperous church he had founded at Corinth. The entire letter, dated somewhere between AD 53 and 57, mixes doctrine and daily practice and includes comments about women covering their heads and not speaking in church. The comments are annoying, even insulting, to the contemporary mind. Though clearly disciplinary and not doctrinal, the passage has been interpreted as forbidding women to preach, teach, or chant during liturgy.[3]

What else does Paul say about women? Introducing his first admonition regarding women covering their heads, Paul explicitly calls it a "tradition" and does not call it a teaching or doctrine. He writes, "Any woman who prays or prophesies with her head unveiled disgraces her head" (1 Cor 11:5). The sentence can be understood to present an implied contradiction with the passage above, which refuses women permission to speak in church, for it requires women to cover their heads when prophesying. Paul writes again:

> Judge for yourselves: is it proper for a woman to pray to God with her head unveiled? Does not nature itself teach you that if a man wears long hair, it is degrading to him, but if a woman has long hair, it is her glory? For her hair is given to her for a covering. But if anyone is disposed to be contentious—we have no such custom, nor do the churches of God. (1 Cor 11:13—16)

The admonition that women must cover their heads when praying is here clearly identified as a "custom." In fact, the

---

3. Regarding women chanting during liturgy, see Susan Ashbrook Harvey, "Performance as Exegesis: Women's Liturgical Choirs in Syriac Tradition," in *Inquiries into Eastern Christian Worship: Acts of the Second International Congress of the Society of Oriental Liturgy*, ed. Basilius J. Groen, Stephanos Alexopoulos, and Steven Hawkes-Teeples, Eastern Christian Studies 12 (Leuven: Peeters, 2012), 47-64.

passage seems to present contradictory requirements in that it admonishes women not to cut their hair or shave their heads, in which case they must be veiled, but then seems to eliminate the requirement for a veil if a woman has long hair.

We know the passage on veiling has been interpreted in various ways; today, it calls to mind certain Middle Eastern and Muslim customs that require women to be veiled, have their heads and sometimes their faces covered, and in some instances, loosely robe their entire bodies. It also echoes contemporary Hasidic and Orthodox Jewish traditions that call for women to cover their heads, sometimes followed by women shaving their heads and wearing wigs or by wearing wigs over their hair and most often by wearing some sort of head covering.

Two additional points must be made here, however, because while many commentators focus on the passage's veiling requirement, the passage provides documentation that the tradition allows women to pray and to prophesize in public. At the very least we can see that the writer's concern here is not the fact of women praying or prophesizing in public, each an oral and audible task, but rather that they demonstrate their submission to God by covering their heads, either with long hair or with a veil.

So, what is one to make of the later comment that women should be silent in churches and that, if they want to know anything, they should ask their husbands at home? In this later passage in Corinthians, Paul cites law as the arbiter of fact: "They are not permitted to speak, but should be subordinate, as the law also says" (1 Cor 14:34). Paul cites law. But is it the law of God or the law of man that silences women in church?

Certainly, the law of man can be invoked here. We know that one of the duties of women deacons was to keep order in the women's portions of the assembly. That translates to keeping the chatter down and perhaps barring men from the area during services. That could suffice to explain Paul's admonition.

Also, the custom of the epoch is reflected, where women, here admonished to get whatever information they need from their husbands at home, were legally subordinate to them. They were not only subordinated; they were his property. Such is still the case in many parts of the world, where women are legally chattel, along with any other property other than real estate.[4]

But is the message of Jesus reflected in the interpretation that women cannot speak at all in the assembly? That is, can this passage be interpreted to mean that women cannot preach, let alone speak, in church at all? The earlier passage from Corinthians clearly admits women to public, oral prayer and to public, oral prophesy. The first passage in Corinthians tells women how they are to appear within the assembly and, by extension, in public. Can these apparently conflicting views be rectified and balanced to recognize the facts of Christianity and the world today? Can these apparently conflicting views be rectified and balanced to recognize the full participation of women in the Church?

We know that from its earliest days, the Church has welcomed women as teachers. We know that the women who assisted in the baptisms of women were their catechists as well. We also know that women were responsible for the catechesis of young people. To argue that women would be restricted from these tasks today is unthinkable. Contemporaneously, in the developed world women frequently are the catechists, both in their families and in their parishes, where they form the backbones of parochial religious education efforts,

---

4. England abolished chattel laws in 1857; only in 1981 did the Republic of Ireland abolish the concept of wifely chattel with the Family Law Act. The United Nations has set 2030 as the target date for the elimination of discriminatory laws and lack of legal protections for more than 50 million women and girls in 100 countries.

and missionary women serve as catechists in many developing nations.

So, today, women are not restricted from catechesis. Except they are and have been. Women are restricted, not only from formal teaching (as homilists), but also from formal involvement in the preparation of catechisms or in the formal acceptance of them on behalf of a territory or diocese for official use. And only in the most recent past have women been accepted to Catholic theological education at pontifical universities. For example, the Pontifical Gregorian University awarded its first doctorates in theology to women in 1975; The Catholic University of America in 1981.[5]

CATECHISMS

Catechisms have historically been within the purview of men: men wrote them, men approved them, men promulgated them.

In the ancient world, the cult of Mithras, an early Greco-Roman mystery religion, competed with early Christianity at least through the fourth century. Mithraism, as it is known, included seven stages of initiation, communal meals, and catecheticals, or lists of teachings.

Early Christianity developed its own lists of teachings, notably by Cyril of Jerusalem (ca. 313–86) and by Augustine of Hippo (354–430), now each a doctor of the Church. Cyril appears to have been born in or near Jerusalem, where he became bishop in the year 350. Augustine, born in Roman North Africa (now Algeria), was bishop of Hippo Regius (also in Algeria) from 396 until his death. Each man presented catechetical teachings, but they did not always agree, mirroring

---

5. Mary Milligan, RSHM, and Sandra M. Schneiders, IHM, at the Gregorian; Elizabeth Johnson, CSJ, at Catholic University.

the differences between Carthage and Alexandria and underscoring the fact that all theology is contextual.

The prologue to Cyril's *Catechetical Lectures* finds him joining Paul in admonishing women to keep silent in church, explaining that Paul's pertinent sentences require women to sit separately from the men and to either sing or read quietly. Cyril cites 1 Timothy 2:12: "I suffer not a woman to speak in church."[6]

However, Augustine's *De Catechizandis Rudibus* (ca. 400), a powerful methodological presentation of doctrine on how and what to teach persons uneducated or inexperienced in the faith, presents no such admonition.

Catechisms were meant to collect teachings in sometimes simplified form so that the uninitiated could be brought into Christianity, sometimes taking one side or the other of a disciplinary question. The catechisms of Cyril and Augustine demonstrate that even in ancient Christianity—clearly not a unified entity—there was discussion about the place of women in teaching and especially in preaching.

We know women deacons taught the faith to newly baptized women and to children, and we can assume these women carried the teachings to their homes and families as well. As the Church grew, its teachings continued to be passed on by women, while its regulations continued to be developed by men.

In later years, from the time of the Reformation onward, Christian catechisms served to present the truths of the faith in a more formal, perhaps more organized, manner. These catechisms were consciously aimed at providing a text so that the teachings of the Church could be transmitted within families, from Luther's *Large Catechism* (1529) to the Reformed or

6. *Prologue to the Catechetical Lectures of Our Holy Father, Cyril, Archbishop of Jerusalem*, para. 14, http://www.newadvent.org/fathers/310100.htm (accessed January 31, 2019).

Geneva Catechism with a preface by John Calvin (1541, 1545, 1560), to the *Heidelberg Catechism* of the Reformed traditions (1562), to the *Westminster Confession of Faith*, which *Larger and Shorter* editions were produced for families and churches (1647). There are many other Reformed catechisms, including the *Basel Catechism* (1526). The Anglican *Book of Common Prayer* (1549) includes a catechetical manual. It is fair to say that all were prepared and approved by men. It is also fair to say that women used them.

Catholic catechisms also came to the fore during the sixteenth century, beginning with the *Roman Catechism* or *Catechism of Pius V*, also known as the *Catechism of the Council of Trent* (1566), aimed at educating clergy in doctrine to alleviate the dual problems of unknowing clergy and consequently uncatechized laity. Jesuit Peter Canisius produced a short *German Catechism*, and the fifty-page *Catechism of Pope St. Pius X* was first published in Italian in 1908. The latter, republished in 1930 with illustrations and important prayers, presented the faith in three sections: Faith, the Ten Commandments, and Grace.

In the United States, several editions of the *Baltimore Catechism* held sway from 1855 through the 1960s, complemented in English by the twentieth-century British *Penny Catechism*. Following the close of the Second Vatican Council, the *Dutch Catechism, De nieuwe katechismus* or *New Catechism* (1966), was an oft-criticized best seller authorized and approved by the hierarchy of The Netherlands. The most recent Catholic catechism is the most complete issued since the Council of Trent and is entitled, simply, *Catechism of the Catholic Church* (1992).

This newest catechism falls into the category of major catechisms, in that it is a universal catechism, intended for the entire Catholic Church. On its promulgation, Pope John Paul II presented it as the point of reference for any other minor or local catechisms that accommodate various situations and cultures, all the while "carefully preserving the unity of faith and fidelity to Catholic doctrine."[7]

The *Catechism of the Catholic Church* has a long consultative history, but from start to finish the process seems to have been overseen by Joseph Cardinal Ratzinger, prefect of the Congregation for the Doctrine of the Faith from 1981 to 2005, when he was elected to the papacy and became Pope Benedict XVI. Following the 1985 Second Extraordinary General Assembly of the Synod of Bishops, which met to consider the twentieth anniversary of the close of the Second Vatican Council, in 1986, Pope John Paul II appointed a panel of twelve cardinals and bishops assisted by seven diocesan bishops. The preparatory commission, under the presidency of then-Cardinal Ratzinger, included Cardinal Jan Pieter Schotte, Secretary General of the Synod of Bishops; Bishop Tarciscio Bertone, SDB, Secretary of the Congregation for the Doctrine of the Faith; Bishop Ternyàk Csaba, Secretary of the Congregation for the Clergy; Cardinal Christoph Schönborn, OP, Archbishop of Vienna; Bishop Claudio Maria Celli, Secretary for the Patrimony of the Apostolic See. In total, some twenty-seven individuals worked on the actual writing of the *Catechism*, including one layman and one woman—he as an editor and she as a secretary.[8] The rest were clerics.

The *Catechism* appeared first in French in 1992 and in English in 1994. In 1997, the official Latin text appeared, requiring modifications to the earlier editions.[9] More consternation arose over the English translation, finally amended to

---

7. John Paul II, Apostolic Constitution *Fidei depositum*, on the publication of the *Catechism of the Catholic Church* (October 11, 1992), para. 3.

8. See http://www.vatican.va/roman_curia/congregations/cfaith/ccc_docu ments/rc_con_cfaith_doc_19920625_informative-ccc_en.html (accessed February 5, 2019).

9. See http://www.scborromeo.org/ccc/updates.htm (accessed November 1, 2019).

remove inclusive language, even where the translation was perfectly correct. The great part of the complaints came from two secondary translators who saw "feminist language," for example, in the translation of *tous les hommes* as "everyone." The second English translators wrote,

> The infusion of "inclusive language" into the text of the *Catechism* was deemed necessary by the translator also for passages quoted from papal and conciliar documents, from the Fathers of the Church, and even from Scripture. Such a transformation is far more than a "translation"; it is an ideological statement.[10]

Years later, their complaints and examples seem a petty intrusion into honest efforts by the first translator or translators to modernize catechetical thought. Even so, the complainants' arguments prevailed, and the more softened outlook on humanity reverted to a strict masculine view.

EXPLAINING THE CATECHISM

In addition to managing the creation of the *Catechism of the Catholic Church*, at the request of Pope John Paul II, Joseph Cardinal Ratzinger also served as president of a special commission to prepare a *Compendium of the Catechism*. The *Compendium* was completed shortly before John Paul II's death, and its introduction is dated as signed by him three days

---

10. Michael J. Wrenn and Kenneth D. Whitehead, "Unfaithful to Truth: Errant Translation of Catechism Is Rejected," *Crisis Magazine*, November 1, 1993, https://www.crisismagazine.com/1993/unfaithful-to-truth-errant-translation-of-catechism-is-rejected. See also Michael J. Wrenn and Kenneth D. Whitehead, *Flawed Expectations: The Reception of the Catechism of the Catholic Church* (San Francisco: Ignatius Press, 1997).

before his death, on March 30, 2005. A few months after his election as Pope Benedict XVI on April 19, 2005, the former Cardinal Ratzinger issued the *Compendium*.[11]

The *Compendium* presents 598 questions and answers regarding matters of faith and morals, expanding the statements of the *Catechism*.[12] Of special interest here is the *Compendium*'s section on holy orders, which conflates the diaconate, an ordained ministry of service, with the priesthood and the episcopate. The *Compendium* summarizes one view of the *Catechism of the Catholic Church* and reinforces the theory of the "unicity of orders." This theory argues that because it is written that Christ chose only men as apostles, only men may now be ordained to the three grades of holy orders: the episcopate (understood to be the successor office to that of the apostles), the priesthood (a relatively late development), and the diaconate (the office that has included women since its inception).[13]

It is important to recall that the presentation of the unicity of orders is a modern accretion on which rests the general argument that women cannot receive the sacrament of order, whereas the earliest restrictions against women were to priesthood. That is, following the Second Vatican Council, those who oppose women in the diaconate argue that the sacrament of ordination known for all three grades of order—episcopacy,

---

11. Benedict XVI, *Moto proprio* for the approval and publication of the *Compendium of the Catechism of the Catholic Church* (June 28, 2005).

12. Ratzinger signed the document on March 20, 2005, shortly before John Paul II's death and his own election as pope. See http://www.vatican .va/archive/compendium_ccc/documents/archive_2005_compendium-ccc _en.html#The Sacraments at the Service of Communion and Mission (accessed December 10, 2019).

13. The unicity of orders theory is found in Gerhard L. Müller, *Priesthood and Diaconate: The Recipient of the Sacrament of Holy Orders from the Perspective of Creation Theology and Christology*, trans. Michael J. Miller (San Francisco: Ignatius Press, 2002); *Priestertum und Diakonat: Der Empfänger des Weihessakramentes in schöpfungstheologischer und christologischer Perspecktive* (Fieiburg: Johannes Verlag, 2000).

priesthood, and diaconate—binds them inextricably one to another. Of course, if it is accepted that women were sacramentally ordained as deacons, the argument can reverse itself to prove that women can be ordained as priest.

Regarding holy orders, the Ratzinger *Compendium* states,

> 333. Who can receive this sacrament?
> 1577—1578
> 1598
> This sacrament can only be validly received by a baptized man. The Church recognizes herself as bound by this choice made by the Lord Himself. No one can demand to receive the sacrament of Holy Orders, but must be judged suitable for the ministry by the authorities of the Church.[14]

Here, the statement "The Church recognizes herself as bound by this choice made by the Lord Himself" is purposefully misleading. The diaconate, a creation of the apostles, as Pope Francis has pointed out, is not related to Christ's choice of men as apostles, nor to the apostles' choice to create the diaconate and their calling forth the persons nominated by the assembly, or to the later convention of ordaining men as priests. The intent here can be twofold: either Ratzinger wished to say diaconal ordination is not sacramental, or he wishes to say that the fact of sacramentality somehow bars women because it is known that Christ chose male apostles, or both.

As recently as September 2015, in speaking to bishops attending the World Meeting of Families in Philadelphia, Pennsylvania, Pope Francis reiterated the distinction between Christ's choice of apostles and the apostles' later calling forth the seven to diaconal service. At the Philadelphia archdiocese's

---

14. *Compendium of the Catechism of the Catholic Church*, chap. 3, para. 333.

Saint Charles Borromeo Seminary, the pope said about the diaconate,

> I have always been struck by how in the early days of the Church the Hellenists complained that their widows and orphans were not being well cared for. The apostles, of course were not able to handle this themselves, so they got together and came up with deacons. The Holy Spirit inspired them to create deacons.[15]

The operative word here is "create." The diaconate is a creation of the early Church. Moreover, the Church (the people of God), not Christ, put forth the individuals generally considered as the first deacons, who were accepted and ratified in their ministry by the apostles' laying on of hands. That they are recorded in Scripture as males (although one person named may be female) does not guide the Church as a choice of Christ. If indeed they all were men, there are ample cultural supports for such a choice. The point is, the Church created the diaconate as a ministry of service, apparently as an ordained ministry of service, which from its earliest days appears to have included women.

What the Church has created the Church can amend or continue.

The *Catechism of the Catholic Church*, which mentions the diaconate only three times, clearly distinguishes the diaconate from the priesthood and the episcopacy. In 2006, Benedict XVI, as Bishop of Rome, alluded to that fact. Speaking to his presbyterate, he asked if it were possible to include women in ministerial service:

---

15. Pope Francis, "U.S. Visit: Meeting with Bishops Attending the World Meeting of Families," *Origins* 45, no. 19 (October 8, 2015): 341–44, at 343.

I would say this is precisely the question. The priestly ministry from the Lord is, as we know, reserved to men inasmuch as priestly ministry is governance in the profound sense that, in fact, it is the Sacrament that governs the Church. This is the decisive point. It is not the man who does something, but the priest faithful to his mission who governs, in the sense that it is the Sacrament, that is, through the Sacrament it is Christ himself who governs[:] whether through the Eucharist or the other sacraments, it is always Christ who presides. However, it is proper to ask whether in this ministerial service—notwithstanding the fact that here Sacrament and charism are one and the same track (*binario*) on which the Church realizes itself—it is not possible to offer more space, more positions of responsibility to women.[16]

The 2006 discussion centered on ministry, but it also touched on governance. Benedict affirmed the participation of women in charity: he named Hildegard of Bingen, Catherine of Siena, and Teresa of Avila and recalled that in the special prayer for priests in the Roman Canon, "*Nobis quoque peccatoribus*," seven women surround him.[17] But at the end of his thought, Benedict asks if women can be included in formal ministry, can the Church not "offer more space, more positions of responsibility, to women?"

For Benedict, formal inclusion in ministry requires ordination, and formal participation in or delegation of governance can only be granted to a cleric. But the conundrum he seems to see, as presented in his *Compendium*, ties the diaconate to the priesthood as if the diaconate were part of the priesthood.

---

16. See https://it.zenit.org/articles/discorso-improvvisato-da-benedetto-xvi -al-clero-romano/. See also Phyllis Zagano, "The Question of Governance and Ministry for Women," *Theological Studies* 68, no. 2 (June 2007): 348–67.

17. Felicity, Perpetua, Agatha, Lucy, Agnes, Cecilia, and Anastasia.

Even so, it is possible that Benedict himself solved the problem with his *motu proprio Omnium in mentem* ("To everyone's attention"), which modified five canons of the 1983 *Code of Canon Law*, including two regarding ordination, canons 1008 and 1009.[18]

The modifications of canons 1008 and 1009 make it clear that the diaconate and the priesthood are separate and distinct orders. Canon 1008 states in part, "They [those ordained] are thus consecrated and deputed so that, each according to his own grade, they may serve the People of God." Canon 1009 adds a new text, a third paragraph to the canon: "Those who are constituted in the order of the episcopate or the presbyterate receive the mission and capacity to act in the person of Christ the Head, whereas deacons are empowered to serve the People of God in the ministries of the liturgy, the word and charity."

However, echoing the Council document *Lumen gentium*, the Dogmatic Constitution on the Church promulgated by Pope Paul VI in 1964, the 1983 *Catechism of the Catholic Church* had already separated the orders. Paragraphs 1562–68 speak to priesthood and priests "bound together by an intimate sacramental brotherhood" that does not include the diaconate. Deacons, however, are ordained "to serve," and "the sacrament of Holy Orders marks them [deacons] with an imprint ('character') which cannot be removed, and which configures them to Christ, who made himself the 'deacon' or servant of all."[19]

Returning to the Ratzinger *Compendium*, we see echoes of the intertwined themes of service and ministry, along with the fact that the deacon is "configured to Christ," that is, the deacon is an icon of Christ:

---

18. See http://w2.vatican.va/content/benedict-xvi/en/apost_letters/documents/hf_ben-xvi_apl_20091026_codex-iuris-canonici.html.

19. *Catechism of the Catholic Church*, para. 1570, citing Mark 10:45 and Luke 22:27; St. Polycarp, *Ad Phil*. 5, 2: SCh 10, 182.

330. What is the effect of the ordination to the diaconate?

1569–1571

1596

The deacon, configured to Christ the servant of all, is ordained for service to the Church. He carries out this service under the authority of his proper bishop by the ministry of the Word, of divine worship, of pastoral care and of charity.

The section poses no challenge to those who accept that women can image the Risen Lord. Early in 2019, however, Cardinal Gerhard Müller, who served as prefect of the Congregation for the Doctrine of the Faith from 2012 until 2017, issued his personal "Manifesto of Faith," joining a small chorus of retired or removed Vatican officials, including cardinals, who object to Pope Francis's theology with increasing anger and disrespect. As a professor of theology and member of the Congregation for the Doctrine of the Faith's second International Theological Commission subcommission on the diaconate, Müller was a guiding force in *From the Diakonia of Christ to the Diakonia of the Apostles,*[20] the 2002 ITC document on the diaconate. That document, originally published in French as *Le diaconat: évolution et perspectives*, replaced and expanded upon a shorter, 1997 International Theological Commission document, which by all accounts agreed that women deacons were sacramentally ordained and could be so ordained again. As Congregation for the Doctrine of the Faith prefect, Cardinal Ratzinger refused to sign the original findings.

Ratzinger reconstituted the International Theological Commission subcommission for its 1997–2002 term, naming

---

20. See http://www.vatican.va/roman_curia/congregations/cfaith/cti_documents/rc_con_cfaith_pro_05072004_diaconate_en.html.

his former graduate student Henrique de Noronha Galvão as its chair and including then-Father Müller. The resultant, longer document found that male and female deacons in antiquity were not identically tasked and said that the Church has long distinguished between the diaconate and the priesthood and that the Magisterium must therefore decide on the question of readmitting women to the ordained diaconate.[21] The reworked document included some eighteen sections or sentences taken or paraphrased from a book by Müller,[22] who appears to have been rewarded for his work nearly immediately: on the document's publication he was named bishop of Regensburg, where he served until being named CDF prefect in 2012, where he served until 2017.[23]

In his personal "Manifesto," Müller interprets sections of the *Catechism* to his own advantage and plainly states that women cannot image Christ:

> "The priest continues the work of redemption on earth" (CCC 1589). The ordination of the priest "gives him a sacred power" (CCC 1592), which is irreplaceable, because through it Jesus becomes

---

21. The original subcommittee, which found in favor of women deacons, was chaired by Msgr. Max Thurian and composed of the following members: H.E. Mgr. Christoph Schönborn, OP, H.E. Mgr. Joseph Osei-Bonsu, Rev. Charles Acton, Mgr. Giuseppe Colombo, Mgr. Joseph Doré, PSS, Prof. Gösta Hallonsten, Rev. Father Stanislaw Nagy, SCI, Rev. Henrique de Noronha Galvão. The second subcommittee, chaired by Rev. Henrique de Noronha Galvão, included Rev. Santiago del Cura Elena, Rev. Pierre Gaudette, Mgr. Roland Minnerath, Mgr. Gerhard Ludwig Müller, Mgr. Luis Antonio G. Tagle, and Rev. Ladislaus Vanyo.

22. Phyllis Zagano, "Ordain Catholic Women as Deacons," *Harvard Divinity Bulletin* 43, nos. 3-4 (Summer/Autumn 2015) : 10-12.

23. Investigations show Müller as bishop of Regensburg was derelict in his oversight of pederast priests and investigating abusive behavior at the Regensburger Domspatzen choir, directed by Ratzinger's older brother, Msgr. George Ratzinger, for thirty years. See https://cruxnow.com/global-church/2017/07/18/hundreds-boys-abused-choir-run-georg-ratzinger/ (accessed December 10, 2019).

sacramentally present in His saving action. Therefore, priests voluntarily opt for celibacy as "a sign
of new life" (CCC 1579). It is about the self-giving
in the service of Christ and His coming kingdom.
With a view to receiving the ordination in the three
stages of this ministry, the Church is "bound by
the choice made by the Lord Himself. That is why
it is not possible to ordain women" (CCC 1577). To
imply that this impossibility is somehow a form
of discrimination against women shows only the
lack of understanding for this sacrament, which is
not about earthly power but the representation of
Christ, the Bridegroom of the Church.

At first, it appears that Cardinal Müller is only excluding women
from priesthood, but on close analysis he clearly calls to all
grades of order, citing as his authority CCC 1577, which, aside
from presenting the current canon 1024 ("Only a baptized man
[*vir*] validly receives sacred ordination") also states that the
apostles chose only men as "collaborators in their ministry"
and notes a long list of Scripture citations.[24] Just one of those
Scripture citations deserves mention here: 1 Timothy 3:1–13,
the passage listing the qualifications for ministry that even the
U.S. Conference of Catholic Bishops agrees refers to women
deacons.[25] Also note that in commenting on the *Catechism*'s
section on the diaconate, the Ratzinger *Compendium* states
that the deacon is "configured to Christ the servant of all."

Two questions arise here: first, the ever-present argument
that women cannot image Christ; and second, the place of the
deacon—should the deacon be female—in divine worship.

It is a historical fact that women deacons catechized, and

---

24. Footnote 67: cf. Mark 3:14-19; Luke 6:12-16; 1 Tim 3:1-13; 2 Tim 1:6;
Titus 1:5-9; St. Clement of Rome, *Ad Cor.* 42, 4; 44, 3; *PG* 1, 292-93; 300.
25. See p. 14 above.

presumably they used catechetical materials where they were available. But in their teachings and in their ministries, how else were women deacons a part of the diaconate? How else did they proclaim the Gospel?

WOMEN PREACHING

The history of women preaching is conflicted and con-flicting. We know that women "preached." In modern times, Benedict XVI and others recall that in the fourteenth cen-tury, it was Catherine of Siena who convinced the French Pope Gregory XI to return to Rome and who later worked to convince the Church that his successor, the Neapolitan Pope Urban VI, was the true pope. The immediate question arises: What is preaching? Can the words of women even be included in this category?

There are many ways of preaching. The recommendation "Preach always, use words if necessary," attributed to Francis of Assisi, is reflected throughout his life story. The saint was—or was not—an ordained deacon. But his "preaching"—his service—was to the people bereft of teachings about Scrip-ture, of material needs, and even not always very welcome at liturgy.

The deacon is charged with the Word, the liturgy, and charity. We can make an argument that women are already included in each of these. Women catechize in various ways. Women celebrate the Liturgy of the Hours and participate in celebrations of the Eucharist. And women are foremost in providing Christian charity. Women are not included in other diaconal tasks and functions, which in some cases they could and can perform through special permission.

Formal preaching—giving homilies—is at the juncture of need and vocation for women. The women who study the

Word, who participate in liturgy, and who minister works of charity are the most obvious candidates to preach the homily at the Mass. But women, in fact all laypersons, cannot preach a homily during the Mass.

The Catholic celebration of Eucharist, the Mass, includes two parts: the Liturgy of the Word and the Liturgy of the Eucharist. The first part of the Mass, the Liturgy of the Word, includes readings from Scripture and a homily. Of these readings, during the week the first is from either the Old Testament or a non-Gospel part of the New Testament, or from each on Sundays, and a Psalm. The Gospel is a reading from one of the evangelists: Matthew, Mark, Luke, or John. In the present discipline in the Western, or Roman Catholic, Church, a lector (formally installed or not) reads the first and second readings and, if there is no cantor, the lector reads the psalm. The deacon or priest participating in the given liturgy (and only a deacon or priest participating in the given Mass) reads the Gospel and preaches a homily.

HOMILIES

The preacher at the Mass is representative of the local ordinary, who is responsible for oversight of all presentation of doctrine in his monastery, territory, or diocese. Ordinarily, there is really no exception for anyone beyond a deacon or priest (again, who is participating in a given Mass) to preach the homily, even though the current interpretation of the guiding canon 766 (limited by canon 767) allows the bishop in certain circumstances, where both necessary and useful, to allow another person to preach. The Norms relative to this canon approved by the U.S. Conference of Catholic Bishops cite the following circumstances: "the absence or shortage of clergy, particular language requirements, or the demonstrated expertise or experience of the lay faithful concerned." The Norms refer not to the Instruction but to a publication of the Pontifical Commission for the Authentic Interpretation of the *Code of Canon Law*:

> The diocesan bishop will determine the appropriate situations in accord with canon 772, §1. In providing for preaching by the lay faithful the diocesan bishop may never dispense from the norm which reserves the homily to the sacred ministers (c. 767, §1; cf. Pontifical Commission for the Authentic Interpretation of the Code of Canon Law, 26 May 1987, in AAS 79 [1987], 1249). Preaching by the lay faithful may not take place within the Celebration of the Eucharist at the moment reserved for the homily.[26]

The Instruction is quick to point out that such preaching, presumably by nonordained lay faithful, may not be considered "an ordinary occurrence, not as an authentic promotion of the laity"; nor may it take place at the ordinary moment of the Mass reserved for the homily.

But the 1997 Instruction refers to canon 766, which already allowed one exception. Buried in a footnote is the reference to the Directory for Masses with Children, *Pueros Baptizatos*, published in 1973 by the Congregation for Divine Worship:[27]

> With the consent of the pastor or rector of the church, one of the adults may speak to the children

---

26. See www.usccb.org/beliefs-and-teachings/what-we-believe/canon-law/com plementary-norms/canon-766-lay-preaching.cfm (accessed December 10, 2019).

27. Sacred Congregation for Divine Worship, Directory for Masses with Children, *Pueros Baptizatos* (November 1, 1973), n. 48: *AAS* 66 (1974).

after the Gospel, especially if the priest finds it difficult to adapt himself to the mentality of children.[28]

Masses celebrated for children may have a lay homilist who can better relate to the children. This exception to the law not only recognizes the fact, anchored in the deepest recesses of the history of the Church, that women routinely catechize children and youth, but the Directory backs away neatly from preferring people (women) better adept at speaking with children than preferred homilists: "In this matter, the Norms soon to be issued by the Congregation for the Clergy should be observed."[29]

So which is it? Can women preach the homily at the reserved time within the Mass when it is a Mass for children? The argument can fall to one side or the other and so, as with so many other matters, the decision seems left to the bishop, or even the pastor or rector of the place where the Mass is celebrated. Whether common sense prevails seems a vagary of person, time, and location.

But we know and well understand that women have always catechized children. The implicit fear regarding the homily is that women might have a different interpretation of Scripture, in addition to the acceptance of Paul's disputed admonition that women cannot speak in Church.

Even though women have always catechized children, they have done so primarily using catechisms prepared by men. Except: The explosive trends of the Second Vatican Council, the increasing numbers of women trained in theology, and the increased access of laypersons to publications of every sort have combined to present a more feminine view of Church teachings to children, youth, and adults. While the classroom was always the place where women (in many parts

28. Op. cit. chap. 3. part 1., no. 24.
29. Op. cit. chap. 3. part 1., no. 24.

of the world, principally women religious) held forth on the teachings of the Church, the postconciliar era saw decreasing numbers of women religious, especially in schools. However, as the teachings of Vatican II filtered to the Church, increasing numbers of women writers and editors at publishing houses were preparing catechetical materials geared more toward the young than the hefty *Catechism of the Catholic Church*. By the time of its 1992 publication, the 581-page French *Catéchisme de l'Église Catholique of the Catholic Church* had already been overtaken by catechetical materials from William H. Sadlier, Inc. in the United States, The Irish Primary Catechetical Programme, and even by the U.S. Conference of Catholic Bishops' National Catechetical Directory, *Sharing the Light of Faith*.[30]

Tied in to classroom catechesis of youth is preaching the homily. In 1997, Pope John Paul II approved and promulgated a jointly written *Instruction on Certain Questions Regarding the Collaboration of the Non-Ordained Faithful in the Sacred Ministry of Priest*.[31]

On the one hand, the jointly promulgated document states at the onset, "The necessity and importance of apostolic

---

30. The U.S. Directory, eight years in preparation, benefited from response to four consultations with dioceses. Mary Charles Bryce, "Religious Education in the Pastoral Letters and National Meetings of the U.S. Hierarchy," in *Sourcebook for Modern Catechetics*, ed. Michael Warren (Winona, MN: Saint Mary's Press, 1983), 261; J. E. Greer, "The Irish Primary Catechetical Programme," *The Furrow* 28, no. 11 (November 1977): 667-78.

31. The Instruction is signed by the prefects of the Congregations for Clergy (Dario Castrillón Hoyos), Doctrine of the Faith (Joseph Ratzinger), Divine Worship and the Discipline of the Sacraments (Jorge Arturo Medina Estévez), Bishops (Bernard Gantin), Evangelization of Peoples (Jozef Tomko), Institutes of Consecrated Life and Societies of Apostolic Life (Eduardo Martinez Somalo), as well as the Pontifical Councils for the Laity (James Stafford) and for the Interpretation of Legislative Texts (Julián Herranz). See http://www.vatican.va/roman_curia/pontifical_councils/laity/documents/rc_con_interdic_doc_15081997_en.html. Three of these signers would collaborate on the later document forbidding the training of women as deacons, Hoyos, Ratzinger, Medina-Estévez.

action on the part of the lay faithful in present and future evangelization must be borne in mind." On the other hand, the document stakes out restricted territory: speaking of "the sacred ministry of the clergy," while confusingly speaking about the "secular character of the lay faithful."

As an aside, perhaps it is well to consider the ways in which Catholic women have been unnecessarily split apart in this regard. All women are laywomen. Some are religious (those belonging to religious institutes or orders); some are secular (all the rest).[32] But no woman is a cleric. No woman, religious or secular, has any greater or less official access to altar service. Of course, the consecrated lives of women religious are lived in specific ways that can better form them for altar service and for preaching, but the altar rail remains a fence beyond which no woman may go, excepting in places where women are permitted to serve as lectors or acolytes. (Laymen and laywomen serve by exception; typically, only men on the path to ordination are formally installed as lectors or acolytes.)[33]

The joint document on lay ministry continues, recognizing and expressing gratitude for the ways in which "numerous religious and lay faithful present themselves" in emergency

---

32. Consecrated virgins, of which there are between four thousand and five thousand worldwide, are attached to dioceses but do not receive benefices or guaranteed employment from their bishops. Some members of religious institutes or orders have received the consecration of virginity. The rite was restored in 1970 and legislated on most recently with the Congregation for Institutes of Consecrated Life and Societies of Apostolic Life Instruction, *Ecclesiae Sponsae Imago* (July 3, 2018), https://press.vatican.va/content/salastampa/en/bollettino/pubblico/2018/07/04/180704d.html.

33. "Canon 230 §2. Lay persons can fulfill the function of lector in liturgical actions by temporary designation. All lay persons can also perform the functions of commentator or cantor, or other functions, according to the norm of law (§3). When the need of the Church warrants it and ministers are lacking, lay persons, even if they are not lectors or acolytes, can also supply certain of their duties, namely, to exercise the ministry of the Word, to preside over liturgical prayers, to confer baptism, and to distribute holy communion, according to the prescripts of the law."

situations, and in situations of "chronic necessity," these due to the "shortage or scarcity of sacred ministers," apparently priests.[34] No matter how helpful, it appears that even when laypersons (secular or religious) are permanently assigned to manage parish affairs (in the United States they are often called pastoral life coordinators), the document is clear in stating that their ministry is an "exercise of tasks," and in italics warns: *"The exercise of such tasks do not make Pastors of the lay faithful."*[35] Here, the document appears to assume only priestly ordination, echoing the teaching that only the priest acts *in persona Christi capitas*:

> *The exercise of such tasks does not make Pastors of the lay faithful*, in fact, a person is not a minister simply in performing a task, but through sacramental ordination. Only the Sacrament of Orders gives the ordained minister a particular participation in the office of Christ, the Shepherd and Head in his Eternal Priesthood. The task exercised in virtue of supply takes its legitimacy formally and immediately from the official deputation given by Pastors, as well as from its concrete exercise under the guidance of ecclesiastical authority. (*Christifedeles laici*; December 30, 1998)

We can return to the restrictions on lay ministry aside from the ministry of the Word, or preaching, which is the topic here. Basically, the document describes ministry of the Word as "the pastoral preaching, catechetics and all forms of Christian

34. Citing John Paul II, Discourse at the Symposium on "The Participation of the Lay Faithful in the Priestly Ministry" (April 22, 1994), n2, *L'Osservatore Romano*, English Edition, May 11, 1994.
35. Quoting John Paul II, Post-Synodal Apostolic Exhortation *Christifedeles laici* (December 30, 1998), n23: *AAS* 81 (1989), 430.

instruction, among which the liturgical homily should hold pride of place."[36] It is immediately apparent that laypersons are not preachers. They may be "heralds of the faith" insofar as catechesis is concerned, but the true task of preaching is reserved to the bishop and through his priests and deacons. As noted above, laypersons ("non-ordained faithful") are permitted to supply for preachers in specific instances, and in no case can such preaching be seen as an ordinary or authentic promotion of the laity. Catechists are reminded that in their own catechesis the "dispensers of the mysteries" are solely the priests. The restriction is due to their having been ordained, from which the bishop cannot validly dispense.

The theological point must be considered here. The document states that the inability of the bishop to give ordinary preaching faculties to a non-ordained person is not a disciplinary law, that is, not a merely ecclesiastical law, "but one which touches on the closely connected functions of teaching and sanctifying." (Recall the triple *munera: munus docendi, munus sanctificandi, munus regendi* [to teach, to sanctify, to rule].) No matter any local practice, the document forbids seminarians and theology students who are not clerics from preaching the homily. Further, any norms that may have admitted laypersons to preaching the homily during the Mass are, according to the document, abrogated by canon 767, paragraph 1. As of 1997, only the ordained may preach a homily, period.

---

36. Citing Second Vatican Council, Dogmatic Constitution *Dei verbum*, n24.

3

ALTAR SERVICE

Hardly anyone, however, now knows what ministerial service women deacons fulfilled in the clerical office at that time....Others say that it was permitted for these women to approach even the holy altar and to go about the [tasks] of the male deacons much like them. But they have been prevented by later Fathers both from ascending to this and from pursuing the [tasks] of this ministerial service because of the involuntary flow of their menses. But that the holy altar was accessible long ago also to women is something that has been inferred from many other things.

Matthew Blastares

PREACHING, SERVICE AT THE ALTAR, and clerical status are inextricably linked.[1]

The homilist typically presents his points from a raised platform or ambo. His permission to preach comes from the

---

1. Much of the research in this chapter appears in Phyllis Zagano, "Women Deacons, Women, and Service at the Altar," *Theological Studies* 79, no. 3 (September 2018): 590-609.

bishop; his perceived authority comes from the elevation of his body and from the stole he wears. He rarely moves beyond the altar rail and, most formally, should not do so. His words emanate from within the sacred precincts of the sanctuary, to which women are now only grudgingly allowed (in certain cultures) to serve as acolytes and lectors.

Service at the altar in the most formal settings includes cassock and surplice-wearing men or boys only: witness celebrations at St. Peter's Basilica. Even though canon 230 of the *Code of Canon Law* permits the bishop to allow laypersons to supply for the formally installed ministries of lector or acolyte, and only laymen may be formally installed to these ministries, there is substantial resistance in the most conservative corners of the liturgical world against women acolytes, even against women lectors. There is matching resistance in the most conservative quarters of the Church at large. Such resistance fulminates despite an overwhelming approval of Proposition 17 of the Twelfth Ordinary General Assembly of the Synod of Bishops in 2008 ("The Word of God in the Life and Mission of the Church") that allows both men and women to be formally installed as lector.[2] The October 2019 Amazon Synod asked for both women lectors and acolytes:

> Seeing the concrete suffering of women who are victims of physical, moral and religious violence, including femicide, the Church commits to defend their rights and recognises them as protagonists

---

2. Proposition 17 of the 2008 Synod of Bishops proposing women be installed as lectors passed with a vote of 191-453 and was forwarded to Pope Benedict XVI. See John L. Allen Jr., "Synod: Final Propositions of the Synod of Bishops on the Bible," *National Catholic Reporter*, October 27, 2008, accessed December 16, 2019, https://www.ncronline.org/news/synod-final-propositions -synod-bishops-bible.

and guardians of creation and of our common home. We recognize the ministry that Jesus reserved for women. It is necessary to promote the formation of women in biblical theology, systematic theology and canon law, valuing their presence in organizations and leadership within the Church environment and beyond. We want to strengthen family ties, especially for migrant women. We assure women's place in leadership and formation. We ask that the Motu Propio of St. Paul VI, *Ministeria quaedam* (1972) be revised, so that women who have been properly trained and prepared can receive the ministries of Lector and Acolyte, among others to be developed. In the new contexts of evangelization and pastoral ministry in the Amazon, where the majority of Catholic communities are led by women, we ask that an instituted ministry of "women community leadership" be created and recognized as part of meeting the changing demands of evangelization and care for communities.[3]

The problem of women, relative to the Word and to altar service, may here rest in the ministry of subdeacon, the major order typically ranked below women deacon (or deaconess) in listings: subdeacon, deaconess, deacon, priest. Some writers argue that this listing of ministries indicates, even proves, that women were not admitted to major orders. Such an argument ignores the fact that the subdiaconate, up to the time of its suppression following Vatican II, has always been under-

---

3. Special Assembly of the Synod of Bishops for the Pan-Amazon Region, "Amazonia: New Paths for the Church and for an Integral Ecology," Final Document of the Special Assembly for the Pan-Amazonian Region, October 27, 2019, para. 102, http://www.sinodoamazonico.va/content/sinodoamazonico/en/documents/final-document-of-the-amazon-synod.html (accessed December 16, 2019).

stood as a major order. (Recall that minor orders were typically conferred in the sacristy; major orders were conferred within the sanctuary. Women deacons were ordained within the sanctuary.)

There is evidence that women performed diaconal altar service. The mere fact of altar service by women substantiates their membership in the major order of deacon, no matter if linguistic custom in certain times and places called them deaconesses. We know that women served as deacons at the altar in the early Church mainly because there were significant complaints against the practice. As early as the fifth century, Pope Gelasius I railed against women "doing what men do" at the altar, no doubt performing the diaconal tasks of preparing the water and wine at the altar for the sacrifice, distributing the precious blood,[4] and otherwise touching sacred cloths and vessels. While Gelasius's objections might appear strange to many people in today's world, they are deadly serious and they perdure.

In fact, it is important not to overlook the fact that even today women are barred from the sacred. Many Catholic dioceses and individual pastors find it unseemly to have women acolytes (of any age) or women lectors, and none formally installs women to these ministries.[5] More importantly, women even now are considered unclean in many cultures.[6] Catholic prohibitions underscore and support such a view. That

---

4. These are specifically diaconal tasks. Today, distribution of Eucharist and ministering the Precious Blood are often delegated, properly to installed acolytes and by exception to lay ministers.

5. The Diocese of Lincoln, Nebraska, formally installs laymen not on the path to priesthood as lectors and acolytes and allows women to serve as readers. It does not permit women to distribute communion during Mass. There are some variations to the prohibition against women at the altar in other U.S. dioceses.

6. Nepalese Hindu women, Australian Aboriginal women, Yap women, Californian Yurok women, Ethiopian Jewish women, and Colombian Páez women are known to be restricted to menstruation huts, which are illegal in some territories.

women have died (along with their children) in freezing cold menstruation huts, that women have died in dowry burnings, that women have died through beatings by their husbands, that women have died in gang rapes by strangers—these are facts of world history not buried in the past. These are facts that pepper daily news reports, that underscore the overall disrespect for women the Church supported and supports by banning women from preaching, from altar service, and from the clerical caste.[7]

BARRED FROM THE SACRED

What is the problem with women at the altar?

We can begin with a view from the fourteenth century. Matthew Blastares was a Byzantine monk, theologian, and canonist. Around 1335, he published a work known as the *Syntagma*, a compilation of then-known ecclesiastical laws. Blastares's work was more accessible than the *Nomocanon* of Photius (ca. 810/820—93), the ninth-century patriarch of Constantinople, remembered as a principal architect of the East-West Schism. Blastares's alphabetically arranged work cites canons from the *Nomocanon*, and it became well-known and well-used, as it presented Church law and civil law where applicable in twenty-four cross-referenced divisions.

---

7. Dowry burning, typically in South Asian nations, occurs when a bride's family refuses to provide additional dowry. Outlawed in various eras since the fifteenth century, this accounts for between 2,500 and 5,000 deaths annually in India, Pakistan, and Bangladesh, as well as in those communities in diaspora elsewhere in the world. Avnita Lakhani, "Bride-Burning: The 'Elephant in the Room' Is out of Control," *Pepperdine Dispute Resolution Law Journal* 5, no. 2 (2005): 249-98; Michael D. Peck, "Epidemiology of Burns throughout the World. Part II: Intentional Burns in Adults," *Burns* 38, no. 5 (August 2012): 630-37. The United Nations reports that 50,000 women are killed by spouses or family members worldwide. *Global Study on Homicide: Gender-Related Killing of Women and Girls*, United Nations Office on Drugs and Crime (2018):

As a commentator on laws, Blastares has something interesting to say about women deacons. From his fourteenth-century vantage point, he wrote,

> Hardly anyone, however, now knows what ministerial service women deacons fulfilled in the clerical office at that time. But there are those who say that they used to minister to those women who were candidates for baptism, since it was not right for the eyes of men to look upon these women when they were being disrobed, since when they were being baptized they were already well-developed sexually. But others say that it was permitted for these women to approach even the holy altar and to go about the [tasks] of the male deacons much like them. But they have been prevented by later Fathers both from ascending to this and from pursuing the [tasks] of this ministerial service because of the involuntary flow of their menses. But that the holy altar was accessible long ago also to women is something that has been inferred from many other things, and especially from the epitaph that the great Gregory the Theologian has composed for his sister.[8]

Blastares pretty much sums it up. Women cannot approach the sacred. They did serve at the altar, much as male deacons did, but later regulations viewed them unsuitable "because of the

---

8. Matthew Blastares, *Syntagma Canonum*, columns 1173-76 (Migne, *PL* 144), trans. Steven D. Smith. St. Macrina the Younger (324-79) is venerated as a deacon in the Orthodox liturgical calendar. Historical restrictions against ordaining women under the age of sixty, or forty-two, or forty are probably intended to include only women without responsibilities to children, and to all post-menopausal women.

involuntary flow of their menses." Women, Blastares reports, were considered unclean. Things have not changed that much.

Not long ago, I heard about a visiting bishop scheduled to celebrate a baccalaureate Mass at a small coed college in the Southeastern United States. When told there would be female students assisting as lectors and acolytes at the Mass, he exclaimed, "No woman is touching my miter." He is still a diocesan bishop. His attitude perdures in too many places and seems embedded for whatever reasons within the minds of many, including those clerics who refuse to allow female acolytes.

Local legislations began to restrict women from the altar early on. Canon 44 of the fourth-century Synod of Laodicea (Phrygia, in present-day Turkey) states, "Women may not go near the altar." The restriction is clear, and it is definite.

As noted above, even Pope Gelasius I (d. 496) complained, presumably about practices among Greek Catholic Churches: "With impatience, we have heard that divine things have undergone such contempt that women are encouraged to serve at the sacred altars, and that all tasks entrusted to the service of men are performed by a sex for which these [tasks] are not appropriate."[9]

It is possible that Pope Gelasius was more interested in asserting his authority over the East and, consequently, over Eastern liturgical practices, than anything else. But Gelasius's

---

9. "Impatienter audivimus, tantum divinarum rerum subiisse despectum, ut feminae sacris altaribus ministrare firmentur, cunctaque non nisi viorum famulatatui deputata sexum, cui non competent, exhibere." J. D. Mansi, *Sacrorum conciliorum nova et amplissima collectio* (Paris, 1901), 8:44, cap. 26. Alternatively translated, "We have heard to our distress that contempt of divine things has reached such a state that women are encouraged to serve at sacred altars (ministrare sacris altaribus) and to perform all the other tasks that are assigned only to the service of men and for which they [women] are not appropriate." Kevin Madigan and Carolyn Osiek, *Ordained Women in the Early Church: A Documentary History* (Baltimore and London: Johns Hopkins University Press, 2005), 186-88.

apparent disgust at Eastern women near the altar seems to have been inherited elsewhere in the West. Later canons, from local synods in present-day Portugal and France, repeated the admonition. However, the repeated legislations by small, local assemblies of Western bishops against women's altar service prove a simple point: at the time these rulings came into being, women, probably women ordained as deacons, were serving at the altar.[10]

Later, sixth-century complaints of bishops in Gaul (France) over the practice of two priests allowing women to "hold the chalices and presume to administer the blood of Christ to the people of God" may indeed have more to do with the fact that the women were, at the very least, traveling companions of the priests.[11] Even so, the growing unease about priests touching women only served to support the ban on women near the sacred. It did not matter if the priests were married to the women involved.

Later in the sixth century, canon 42 of the *Capitula Martini*, the systematic collection of canon law emanating from Braga (Portugal), states, "Women are not permitted to enter the sanctuary."[12]

It is certain, however, that throughout the early Church women continued to be ordained as deacons, and, one can assume, these ordained women deacons were able to serve as deacons of the Mass. Soon, however, continuing legislations and concomitant complaints often centered on women, ordained or not, being forbidden to distribute communion or

---

10. L. J. Johnson, ed., *Worship in the Early Church: An Anthology of Early Sources* (Collegeville, MN: Liturgical Press, 2010), 2:298–302 at 302. These synodal canons appear in both Greek and Latin.

11. "Letter of Three Gallic Bishops," in Madigan and Osiek, *Women in the Early Church*, 188–90.

12. Johnson, *Worship in the Early Church*, 4:168–9, citing *Opera Omnia*, ed. C.W. Barlow, *Papers and Monographs of the American Academy in Rome* (New Haven, 1950), 12:124ff.

to touch sacred linens and vessels. The accepted "impurity" of women caused canons to pile up, so that a small diocesan synod of Auxerre decreed in the late sixth century, "Women are not to receive the Eucharist in an uncovered hand" (canon 36) and "Women are not to touch the Lord's pall" (canon 37).[13]

Clearly, if a woman—even a woman deacon—is not permitted within the sanctuary, the possibility of her proclaiming the Gospel and preaching is closed. Recall, only a cleric participating in a given Mass is permitted to proclaim the Gospel and to preach. As other liturgical reading became the privileged duty of the subdeacon, and since women never participated in the *cursus honorum*, women's voices and presence in the sanctuary, especially during the Mass, and eventually always, ended in different times in different places.

One slight digression into the facts about "ordination" here regards the synod of Auxerre. Recall that there has been much discussion about whether women deacons were ordained or blessed. The short answer is: both. The terms "blessed," "ordained," "consecrated" were often used interchangeably in the early Church. Canon 21 of the synod of Auxerre, for example, states that a priest once blessed (*une fois reçue la bénédiction*) cannot sleep in the same bed with his wife or "unite with her by the sin of the flesh." The same stricture applies to the deacon and the subdeacon.[14] Two points here: (1) "blessed" and "ordained" are interchangeable terms; and (2) the deep-rooted argument against women clearly includes the notion that intimate touching of women makes a man unclean, thereby rendering him unable to perform the

---

13. L. Duchesne, *Christian Worship: Its Origins and Evolution* (New York: E. & J. B. Young, 1903), 224-25, Auxerre C. 36: "Non licet mulieri nuda manu eucharistism accipere." Also, Johnson, *Worship in the Early Church*, 4:159-61.

14. Jean Gaudemet and Brigitte Basdevant, eds., *Les Canons de Conciles Mérovingiens (VI-VII Siècles)*, Sources Chrétiennes 353, 354 (Paris: Les Éditions du Cerf, 1989), 10:495.

Altar Service

sacrifice or, it seems, even enter the sanctuary. That being the case, one can assume the same stricture would apply to women, before or after their diaconal ordinations, precisely because of their inborn unclean states. That is, no matter that a woman is ordained, she is still innately unclean and therefore cannot enter the sanctuary or be near the holy.

Restrictions continued to pile up against women banned from being near the sacred, especially during the Mass but including during preparations for the liturgical celebration. Concurrently, other regulations appeared levied against abbesses' performing their proper jurisdictional duties: they cannot bless, absolve, teach, or judge; they may read the Gospel at Matins but not during the Mass. Recall, proclaiming the Gospel is a diaconal task, and from time to time and place to place, abbesses were ordinarily ordained as deacons. Even if not ordained as deacons, one would assume that the jurisdictional rights of the abbess would remain.[15]

The question of women at the altar perdured, at least to the eighth century, when Pope Zachary, who reigned from 741 to 752, received an inquiry from Frankish authorities as to whether women (nuns) could read the Gospel at Mass. His answer was no. It remains unclear whether the question revolved around their non-ordained status, although Zachary continued that "as we have heard to our dismay, divine worship has fallen into such disdain that women have presumed to serve the sacred altars... and perform all the things assigned exclusively to men."[16]

---

15. See J. H. Martin, "The Ordination of Women and the Theologians in the Middle Ages," in *A History of Women and Ordination*, ed. Bernard Cooke and Gary Macy (Latham, MD: Scarecrow, 2002), 1:46, citing *Glossa ordinaria on Decretum*, causa 27, q. 1, c. 23 v. Ordinari (Ferrario and Franzino, 1:1973).

16. *Epistola 7, Zachariae Papae Ad Pipinum Majorem Domus, Itemque Ad Episcopos, Abbates, et Proceres Francorum* (Migne, *PL* 89.933C, Jaffe, 2277 [1750], "Gaudio magno," 1:266; trans. in Ute E. Eisen, *Women Officeholders in Early Christianity: Epigraphical and Literary Studies*, trans. Linda Maloney [Collegeville, MN: Liturgical Press, 2000], 133–34).

Soon enough, Haito, the bishop of Basel (in present-day Switzerland), ruled that "women should have no access to the altar and are not to join in any ministry of the altar, even if dedicated to God," thereby making it clear that the problem was neither lay status nor a lack of jurisdiction but only the fact of being female that kept women from the sacred.[17]

Again, one must consider the fact that the regulations are honored only in their breach. If women were not serving at the altar, if women were not even serving as sacristans, then why would there be need for additional laws? That is, if the then-current culture accepted women's altar service, why was it continually rejected? The answer is perhaps embedded in the development of a clerical culture that insisted on its own prerogatives, which continually and increasingly built a wall between itself and the people of God.

WOMEN ARE UNCLEAN

The 829 Council of Paris shored up restrictions against women; its documents complain that some bishops were allowing women's participation in the Mass and thereby blaming them for "illegal feminine access" to the altar. Of course, the complaints provide additional incidental support for the notion that women performed the liturgical tasks of male deacons.[18] The Council documents, which speak for a larger area than the immediate territory around Paris, are clear:

> In some provinces, in contradiction to the divine
> law and to canonical instruction, women betake

---

17. Haito of Basle, *Capitula ecclesiastica*, c. 16, in *Capitularia regum Francorum*, ed. Alfred Boretius, vol. 1, MGH (Hannover: Hahn, 1883), 364.

18. Cap. 45, *Concilium Parrisiense A. 829*, ed. Albert Werminghoff, Concilia aevi Karolini (742–842), Teil 2 (Hannover: Hahn, 1908), 639–40.

themselves into the altar area and impudently take hold of the sacred vessels, hold out the priestly garments to the priest, and what is still worse, more indecent and unfitting than all this—they give the people the body and blood of the Lord and do other things which in themselves are indecent.[19]

One can only imagine what comprises the "other things which in themselves are indecent." In today's mind, the word *indecent* modifies improper, even obscene, actions or inappropriate behavior. If something is indecent it can be dirty, rude, or wicked; it may also be unseemly, improper, indecorous, or unbecoming. Think here of that complaining bishop: No woman was touching his miter! Why?

The strictures of the Council of Paris (829) also decreed that priests and women be kept separate (canon 42), a ruling repeated years later at the Council of Aix-la-Chapelle (Council of Aachen; 836) (canon 6).[20] Obviously, women could not be admitted to the sanctuary during liturgies, or to the sacristy, if they are to be "kept separate" from men, although these regulations seem to be more about regulating priestly celibacy. Even so, it appears that women performing the diaconal tasks of chanting or proclaiming the Gospel, commingling the water and wine for the celebration of Eucharist, and touching sacred vessels or linens could, according to the Council of Paris, fall under the general category of "indecent" actions.

These admonitions were dutifully reported to the Frankish emperor at the time: "We have sought by all possible ways to prevent the illicit admission of women to the altar...[because] women must not enter the altar area is written in the Council

---

19. Cap. 45, *Concilium Parrisiense A. 829*, 639.

20. The Councils of Mayence (847) and Worms (868) supported priests' separation from women, including their sleeping in a common dormitory. André Lagarde, *The Latin Church in the Middle Ages*, 387, 399.

of Chalcedon and in the decrees of Pope Gelasius."[21] The reference to Chalcedon is curious, since the only decree of the Council of Chalcedon (451) referring to women deacons stipulates: "No woman under forty years of age is to be ordained a deacon, and then only after close scrutiny." The Council further stipulates that should she then marry "after receiving ordination," both she and her spouse are to be anathematized, which ruling would indicate her clerical status.[22]

Even so, Gelasius's papal authority, by this time several centuries old, is invoked as ruling against women in the sanctuary. Here, a ninth-century local synod in the West is deferring to a fifth-century pope, the third and presumably the final pope of Christian West African descent.[23] That Pope Gelasius is invoked as definitive ruler in the matter of women at the altar in the Western Church is interesting in two respects: First, it is probable that the women Gelasius complained about in Sicily were following Eastern rubrics; and therefore, second, we can see an attempt now by the Council of Paris to apply to Western liturgy the same strictures Gelasius wished to impose on Eastern liturgy.

The expansion of restrictions against women's altar service here may be better examined by psychologists, but to the modern eye, this expansion could appear to be rooted in the notion that women are wicked temptresses who might put a priest's chastity at risk and whose very presence renders a space unclean. But how many bishops followed Gelasius's ruling over the ensuing years? If for several centuries the ban on

---

21. *Monumenta Germaniae Historica*, Legum Sectio 2 Capitularia regum Francorum (Hanover: Hahn, 1883), vol. 1 (Quarto-Ausgabe) 55, 364 quoted in H. van der Meer, *Women Priests in the Catholic Church?* (Philadelphia: Temple University Press, 1973), 95, 184n38ff.; Conc. Paris, lib. I, c. 45.

22. Norman P. Tanner, *Decrees of the Ecumenical Councils*, vol. 1 (Washington, DC: Georgetown University Press, 1990), 54.

23. Victor I (papacy: 189-99), Miltiades (papacy: 311-14), and Gelasius I (papacy: 492-96) were Christian Berbers.

women's altar service was repeatedly decreed, then why was it repeatedly recalled? The ban, first known to have come from Gelasius following the Synod of Laodicea, must have been ignored.

Also, if women were unclean and at times and in places were refused permission to touch sacred items, let alone take the Eucharist in their hands, how is it that parts of the Church in the West enjoyed the ministry of women carrying the Eucharist to sick women? Southern Italy knew of that practice toward the end of the ninth century, at least among its Greek Churches. There is documentation that Leo, bishop of the ancient diocese Calabria, asked the patriarch of Constantinople how to provide ministry to ill women. Photios, the same ninthcentury patriarch who ruled against nuns chanting the Gospel, replied that the bishop should choose either chaste older women or virgins "worthy of being received into the diaconate and of being received into the rank of deacons." Photius thereby instructed the bishop that women such as he described could be admitted to the diaconate, which order still was known and accepted.[24]

CLERICAL CELIBACY AND MISOGYNY

However influential the Greek Church was in Italy, Byzantine domination (but not influence) ended around the eleventh century. Hence, the Eastern tradition of married clergy—defended and defined at the seventh-century Council

---

24. Valerie Karras, "Female Deacons in the Byzantine Church," *Church History* 73 (2004): 272-315 at 278, citing Ep. 297, 4; in Photios, *Photii patriarchae Constaninopolitani epistulae et amphilochia*, ed. B. Laourdas and L. G. Westerink, Bibliotheca Scriptorum Graecorum et Romanorum Teubneriana (Leipzig: BSB B.G. Teubner, 1983), 3:166. Karras also points out that canonical and legal legislation routinely uses the masculine *diakonos* for Eastern women deacons (280n36).

of Trullo—could have largely disappeared by then, especially given that Greek Catholicism was predominantly lived within and through monasteries. Excepting small enclaves in Southern Italy and in Venice, Greek culture, and therefore traditions of the Eastern Church, would by then have become faded memories.[25]

Concurrently, in the West the stricture of clerical celibacy continued to be enforced, in part as a means of ensuring the "cleanliness" of clerics, especially those who would celebrate the sacrifice of the Mass. The "sin of the flesh" so amply decried at Auxerre was applied to all who wished to be clerics. Once admitted to major orders, they could not be married; if they were married (and some were), they were admonished not to have marital relations with their wives.

Successive councils, from the fourth through the seventh centuries affirmed the Roman discipline restricting celibates to major orders (subdeacon, deacon, priest, bishop) or to not having marital relations with their wives if they were married. Through the eighth and ninth centuries, councils decried clerical immorality, until the ninth century saw an upswing in clerical marriages as a means of ending or at least containing clerical debauchery, and by the tenth century it all but disappeared in Rome and elsewhere in Italy. The continued discussion surrounded benefices and inheritances: clerical fathers would want to provide for their families.

By the beginning of the eleventh century, Peter Damian (ca. 1007/21—1072/3), was calling women the "appetizing flesh of the devil."[26] Peter, a Benedictine monk known

---

25. The Norman invasion of Sicily in the eleventh century resulted in the forced Latinization of Italo-Greek Churches. Albanian refugees revived Byzantine practices in the fifteenth century, and in 1742, with *Etsi pastoralis*, Benedict XIV ratified Greek practices and said these churches should be free from Latin intervention. The Italo-Albanian Church is one of twenty-three Eastern churches in full communion with Rome and has married clergy.

26. Gary Macy, "Impasse Passé: Conjugating a Tense Past," *Proceedings of*

as a reformer, wrote widely against clerical vices, including debauching underage children. Concurrently, there were additional attempts to enforce the rule of celibacy. The Roman Council of 1049 sent the wives of clerics to slavery; a second council a year later forbade laity contact with married priests; and a third council in 1059 forbade attendance at the Masses celebrated by married priests.

Continued legislation through the eleventh century, in Rome, France, England, and other parts of Europe, gradually eroded the legal vestiges of the married clerical state. Ireland remained exceptional, at least through part of the twelfth century, even as the Second Lateran Council (1139) was decreeing against men who were to be "temples of God and sanctuaries of the Holy Spirit" giving themselves up to "marriage and impurity."[27] By the time the 1917 *Code of Canon Law* was promulgated, priests who married were excommunicated.[28]

Successive centuries saw local councils further attempting to assert a rule of celibacy on Latin priests, despite continued dissoluteness among them. The bulk of the legalities were involved with the protection of Church property, even as the terms then and in retrospect center on the "reform" of the clergy, that is, keeping them away from women, contact with

---

the Catholic Theological Society of America 64 (2009): 1-20 at 10-11, citing Anne Barstow, *Married Priests and the Reforming Papacy: The Eleventh-Century Debates*, Texts and Studies in Religion 12 (New York: Edwin Mellon, 1982), 60-61. See also Barstow, *Married Priests*, 47-104; Dyan Elliott, "The Priest's Wife: Female Erasure and the Gregorian Reform," in *Medieval Religion: New Approaches*, ed. Constance Berman (New York: Routledge, 2005), 102-22 at 136-45.

27. Second Lateran Council, Canon 6.

28. Canon 2388 §1. Clerici in sacris constituti vel regulares aut moniales post votum sollemne castitatis, itemque omnes cum aliqua ex praedictis personis matrimonium etiam civiliter tantum contrahere praesumentes, incurrunt in excommunicationem latae sententiae Sedi Apostolicae simpliciter reservatam; clerici praeterea, si moniti, tempore ab Ordinario pro adiunctorum diversitate praefinito, non resipuerint, degradentur, firmo praescripto can.188, n. 5. 1917 *Codex Iuris Canonicis*.

whom would render the cleric unclean. Thirteenth-century commentary by Henricus de Segusio (Hostiensis), a cardinal and professor of law, argues the inferiority of women, while Bernard of Botone presents women as innately stupid.[29]

Misogyny continued to be codified. Women could not be near clerics and certainly not near them in the celebration of Eucharist. Gratian's new decretals in 1240 (*Nova Compilatio decretalium*) added energy to the dismissive attitude toward women, which a century later found Pope Gregory IX stating, "Also, care must be taken that no woman presumes to walk to the altar or to minister to the priest or to stand or to sit within the chancel."[30] Three strands of the discussion continued to intertwine: first, women were argued to be unclean, in addition to being pronounced both temptresses and stupid; second, clerical celibacy in the West was supported by misogyny but revolved around property; and third, the clerics in the East (and Eastern Churches in general) seemed to ignore each of these strictures.

In the thirteenth century, Innocent IV admonished what appears to be the practice in Greek Churches regarding women, perhaps women deacons. In a letter to his legate, Odo of Tusculum, he said, "Women should not dare to serve at the altar; they should be altogether refused this ministry."[31]

---

29. "What is lighter than smoke? A breeze. What [is lighter] than a breeze? The wind. What [is lighter] than the wind? A woman. What [is lighter] than a woman. Nothing!" Macy, "Impasse Passé," 13, citing text in Ida Raming, *Auschluss der Frau vom priesterlichen Amt: Gottgewollte Tradition oder Diskiminierung?* (Cologne, 1973), 149n102; English translation in Raming, *A History of Women and Ordination*, vol. 2, *The Priestly Office of Women: God's Gift for a Renewed Church* (New York: Scarecrow Press, 2004).

30. Corpus Iuris Canonici, c. 1, X, de cohabitatione clericorum et mulierum, III, 2, Friedberg, vol. 2, 454. Cited in van der Meer, *Women Priests*, 97, 184n45.

31. "Mulieres autem servire ad altare non audeant, sed ab illius ministerio repellantur omnino." Innocent IV, Epistole *Sub Catholicae Professione* ad Episcop Tusculanum, Ap. Sefis Legatum apud Graecos (March 6, 1254), accessed December 4, 2017, http://w2.vatican.va/content/innocentius-iv/la/documents/

Soon, the English Dominican theologian at Oxford, Richard Fishacre (ca. 1200–1248), argued against women's altar service, this time using fictional support both to deny the ordination of women deacons (which would automatically deny them access to the altar) and to argue against women touching the sacred:

> If it is asked about those religious women who are called deaconesses, I answer that they are not so called because they share orders with a deacon, but only in so far as they share in some of his offices, *viz.*, because they are permitted to read the Gospel and other readings although it is not allowed to them to touch the sacred vessels as a deacon. Thus, in distinction 23 [*Decretum*, dist. 23, c. 25] Pope Soter to the bishops of Italy, "It has been brought to the attention of the apostolic see that women consecrated to God, or nuns, touch the sacred vessels or blessed palls, that is in the presence of your company, and carry incense around the altar. That all this is blameworthy conduct to be fully censured can be rightly doubted by no wise person. Because of this, by the authority of this Holy See, lest this disease spread more widely, we order all provinces to most swiftly drive it out."[32]

---

epistola-sub-catholicae-professione-6-martii-1254.html. Tusculum is a now ruined city in the Alban Hills four miles south of Frascati. Odo, a Cistercian of Châteauroux and cardinal bishop of Frascati from 1244–73, was a papal legate of Innocent IV. Acolytes are documented since the third century, but there does not seem to be a history of women acolytes.

32. "Si queritur de monialibus que dicuntur diaconisse: Respondeo, non sic dicuntur quia communicent cum diacono in ordine, sed tantum in aliquo eius officii, scilicet quia licenciantur ad legendum Evangelium et dictioni aliquo. Quia non licet eis sacra vasa tangere ut diacono. Unde D. 23 (c. 25). Sother Papa episcopis Italie, 'Sacratas Deo faminas vel monachas sacra vasa vel sacratas pallas, id est corporales, penes vos contingere, et incensum circa altaria deferre,

Fishacre's testimony would be interesting, if true. The statement afforded Pope Soeter is fictional, perhaps even a creation contemporary to Fishacre's writing. Even so, Fishacre appears to accept that there are women at least called deacons—or deaconesses—and yet decries the possibility of their touching anything involved with the Mass. Further, the fictional comment by Soeter that Fishacre uses to substantiate his argument calls women's altar service—women "touch the sacred vessels or blessed palls...and carry incense around the altar"—a "disease." Is further testimony of misogyny needed? Is deeper research into the attitudes prevalent among clerics needed?

Meanwhile, the tug-of-war regarding celibacy continued across Europe, even to Sweden and, again, to Ireland. In 1541, Charles V, the Holy Roman Emperor, wrote that he favored priestly marriage; in 1548, he decreed that married priests could remain so at least until the Council pronounced authoritatively; and in 1560, his successor, Ferdinand, called marriage the only remedy to the corrupt priesthood.[33]

Yet, despite centuries of argumentation about (and outright disregard of) celibacy laws, the Council of Trent, at its twenty-fourth session in 1563, pronounced clerical celibacy an article of faith:

> How shameful a thing, and how unworthy it is of
> the name of clerics who have devoted themselves
> to the service of God, to live in the filth of impurity,

perlatum est ad apostolicam sedem, quo omnia vituperatio reprehensione plena esse nulli recto sapientium dubium est, quia propter huius sancte sedis auctoritate ne pestis hec latius divulgetur, quod ornnes provincias abstergi citissime mandamus.'" Richard Fishacre, *Sentencias Commentaria*, vol. 4, dist. 24; Balliol Ms. 57 (University of Oxford, Balliol College); Oriel Ms 43 (University of Oxford, Oriel College). The *False Decretals* are attributed to late ninth-century Frankish clerics.

33. See "Ecclesiastical Celibacy," in Andre Lagarde, *The Latin Church in the Middle Ages*, trans. A. Alexander (New York: Scribner's Sons, 1915), 382-414.

and unclean bondage, the thing itself doth testify, in the common scandal of all the faithful, and the extreme disgrace entailed on the clerical order. To the end, therefore, that the ministers of the Church may be recalled to that continency and integrity of life which becomes them.[34]

If the cleric maintains his "concubine," he is to be dismissed from the clerical state; if he does not "put away" the woman permanently, he is to be excommunicated.[35]

In 1566, Pius V directed all diocesan bishops to enforce the conciliar ban against concubinage, thereby declaring clerical celibacy obligatory.[36]

It would appear the enforcement of clerical celibacy further supported and was supported by the clerical attitude that women are both "temptresses" and unclean throughout the modern era. While in the seventeenth century, Jean Morin had found (by examination of liturgies) that women were indeed ordained, even according to the criteria of the Council of Trent, by the eighteenth century a new opinion appeared. Jean Pien disagreed with Morin and denied his conclusions.[37]

Pien presented a finding that women could not be ordained. The argument that women cannot be ordained, that is, they are innately incapable of receiving ordination, perdures to this day without any logical support. Such is especially the

34. "Decree on Reformation," Twenty-Fifth Session, ch. 14, *The Council of Trent: The Canons and Decrees of the Sacred and Oecumenical Council of Trent*, ed. and trans. J. Waterworth (London: Dolman, 1848), 271.

35. "Decree on Reformation," Twenty-Fifth Session, ch. 14, 271.

36. H. C. Lea, *History of Sacerdotal Celibacy in the Christian Church*, 3rd rev. ed. (New York: Macmillan, 1907), 2:223.

37. Jean Morin, *Commentarius de sacris ecclesiae ordinationibus secundum antiquos et recentiores latinos, graecos, syros et babylonios in tres partes distinctus* (1655, 1695; reprt. Farnborough: Gregg, 1969); Jean Pien, *Tractatus Praeliminaris de Ecclesiae Diaconissis*, in J. Bollandus et al., eds., *Acta Sanctorum*, September, I, i-xxviii (Antwerp: Bernard Albert Vander Plassch, 1746).

case when considering that men deacons and women deacons were ordained in identical or at least very similar ceremonies at various times and places in Church history. In any event, if women were neither ordained as deacons nor progressing at any stage in the *cursus honorum* as acolytes, lectors, or sub-deacons, they would have no place within the sanctuary during the celebration of the Mass or, in many territories, at any other time.

Around the time of Pien's eighteenth-century negative findings regarding the ordinations of women as deacons, two popes—Clement XII and Benedict XIV—looked to Gelasius (fifth century) and to Innocent IV (thirteenth century) to find support for their banning women from the altar. Benedict XIV called it "the evil practice which had been introduced of women serving the priest at the celebration of Mass."[38] The contemporary eye stares incredulously at the language—a pope is calling female participation in the celebration of Eucharist "evil"—and one can only assume the reasons for such papal vitriol. How much misogyny resided in the papal palace in the eighteenth century?

MODERN MISOGYNY

Although it seems to have begun in the sixteenth century, by the 1700s when Clement XII and Benedict XIV reigned, the *querelle des femmes* still raged in parts of Europe. Women had been claimed by some to be a different species from men. John Knox wrote *The First Blast of the Trumpet against the Monstrous Regiment of Women*, albeit anonymously, in 1558, attacking female monarchs. For Knox, feminine rule was contrary to the Bible.[39]

---

38. Benedict XIV, Encyclical *Allatae Sunt* (July 26, 1755), para. 29.

39. "I am assured that God has revealed to some in this our age, that it is

In general, women were affirmed as less intelligent, less capable, and less able in every respect. In fact, women were considered essentially defective. So, despite hundreds of years of intellectual discussion and defense of women, ranging from the writings of Christine de Pizan (1364–ca. 1430) to those of Mary Wollstonecraft (1759–97), Benedict XIV was able to call feminine participation in the Mass "evil." While the writing of Pizan and Wollstonecraft, and of so many others in the intervening centuries could be negatively styled as "feminist" even by contemporary men, they and many others argue on behalf of the anthropological equality of men and of women. Men and women are equal, if not the same.

Again, by the eighteenth century, the "evil practice" of women serving at the Mass—whether by ordained or non-ordained women is unclear—seems to be blamed on or mostly limited to the Greek Churches. However, in Basque Country here were substantial numbers of *seroras*, women whose permanent ecclesiastical positions in shrines required management of the sacristy and, at the very least, the preparation of the altar for the celebration of Mass.[40] By the beginning of the eighteenth century, however, their work, known since the fifth century, was termed "scandalous."[41] Additionally, keeping women out of the sanctuary was an interest connected to the papal preference for Latin rites, particularly in areas where women were known to somehow have been included in Greek rites.

Meanwhile, papal fulmination continued against married clergy and clergy who otherwise lived with women, as Eastern

---

more than a monster in nature that a woman shall reign and have empire above man." John Knox, *The First Blast of the Trumpet against the Monstrous Regiment of Women*, 1558.

40. Amanda L. Scott, "Community, Conflict and Local Authority: The Basque *Seroras*," in *Devout Laywomen in the Early Modern World*, ed. Alison Weber (London: Routledge, 2016), 31–47.

41. P. Lepe, *Constituciones synodales antiguas y modernas del Obispado de Calahorra y la Calzada* (Madrid, 1700), vol. 3, tit. 12, folio 497.

Churches supported the "unclean" nature of marital relations by regulating those of their own married priests. Bans on marital relations between Eastern married priests and their wives ranged from three to eight days prior to celebrating Eucharist to, in some cases, three to eight days following the celebration. (Note the postcelebration similarity between an eight-day ban and the time after childbirth a woman was "churched.")

Several Eastern Churches maintained their traditions of women deacons, although their liturgical duties were increasingly restricted to monastic liturgies outside the Mass. A major portion of the Vatican Library's manuscript collections from the East (especially Syria, Jerusalem, and Egypt) was collected in the early eighteenth century by Joseph Assemani, whom Clement XII appointed papal visitator to the 1736 Holy Synod of Mount Lebanon. The synod met in an attempt for the Maronite Church to gain more positive recognition from Rome (it never formally broke away during the schism). The synod canons Assemani brought to Rome (in Latin) and formally approved *in forma specifica* by Pope Benedict XIV both advise bishops they may ordain women as deacons and detail these women's duties.[42] Shortly before his death, Clement XII appointed Assemani the first Vatican librarian. Did Assemani, first a Maronite priest before becoming a Latin priest, share Clement's antipathy toward women? Perhaps that might account for the dearth of ancient liturgies in the Vatican Library for ordaining women as deacons, although one Syrian liturgy for ordaining women deacons is deposited there.[43]

The post-Enlightenment period has not brought many

42. Phyllis Zagano, "Women Deacons in the Maronite Church," *Theological Studies* 77 (2016): 593–602.

43. The Vatican Apostolic Library holds three liturgies for ordaining women deacons from the East: Barberini gr. 336 (780), Vatican Manuscript gr. 1872 (1100), and the Codex Syriacus Vaticanus No. 19 (1550). It holds two from the West: Vatican Reginae lat. 337 (850) and the Ottobonianus lat. 313, Paris (850).

changes in official Church teaching regarding women's altar service in the West. In 1901, *Dictionnaire de Droit Canonique*, a French dictionary of canon law, notes that no woman, including a woman in public vows, may cense the altar nor touch sacred vessels nor serve Mass. The dictionary submits that St. Paul's dictum that women may not speak in the assembly means women are forbidden to voice the responses in the Mass. Obviously, women are forbidden from entering the sanctuary due to the combined problems of their innate impurity and the possibility of their distracting the priest. Interestingly, while the dictionary argues that women ordained as deacons do not receive the "imprint of order," it cites Epiphanius's fourth-century instruction that neither male nor female deacons are part of the priesthood.[44]

The universal promulgation of the 1917 *Code of Canon Law* codified the restriction of women from the altar: "The server at Mass should not be a woman, unless no man can be had, and provided the woman stays at a distance to answer the prayers and does not in any way approach the altar."[45]

The deep-seated restriction of women from the sanctuary remains in instructions as well as in custom. *Musicam sacram*, the document on sacred music, issued following the close of Vatican II, remains in effect: "Whenever the choir also includes women, it should be placed outside the sanctuary (presbyterium)."[46]

As for liturgical service, the 1983 *Code of Canon Law* changed the restriction against women's altar service somewhat

44. "L'ordre n'imprime sur elle aucun caractère." "Diaconesses," in *Dictionnaire de Droit Canonique*, 2:633.

45. Canon 813 §1.

46. Second Vatican Council, *Musicam sacram*, Instruction on Music in the Liturgy (March 5, 1967), para. 22. Also: "The choir can consist, according to the customs of each country and other circumstances, of either men and boys, or men and boys only, or men and women, or even, where there is a genuine case for it, of women only."

with canon 230: Bishops can do what they wish regarding altar servers and lector, but the cultural restrictions against women inside the sanctuary remain in various parts of the world and in individual dioceses in otherwise less misogynistic cultures.

4

SPIRITUAL DIRECTION & CONFESSION

> Therefore confess your sins to one another, and
> pray for one another, so that you may be healed.
>
> James 5:16

WOMEN DEACONS IN THE EARLY Church often served as confessors and spiritual companions. Deacons no longer receive faculties for confession, but women in the Church today are spiritual directors.

There is no direct connection between the ordained diaconate and spiritual direction, but the fact of ordination, certainly as priest but also as deacon, can be a determining factor in allowing individuals to obtain permanent employment in a parochial or chaplaincy setting. That is important, because permanent employment in a parish or chaplaincy generally includes professional office space in which to practice spiritual direction, as well as the support net of institutional liability insurance.

Throughout history and even today, the term "spiritual direction" has had wide and varied meanings. Its practice is similarly wide and varied. At its most basic meaning, for an individual to engage in spiritual direction means sharing his or her life of prayer with another person, presumably one further along the road of life with God. The director mainly listens, sometimes affirming, sometimes correcting, sometimes challenging. While the practice of spiritual direction can include the giving of advice, that advice would be directed principally at the practice of prayer and of living one's life with God, while accounting for relationships with self and with others.

The human triad of relationships—God, self, others—is always at the core of any spiritual direction conversation, but spiritual direction is not counseling or psychotherapy. Neither is it the practice of confession or reconciliation. Spiritual direction is aimed at assisting individuals to see God's action in their lives and to help them to respond gratefully and generously.

For Christians, Jesus was the first spiritual director and he remains as the central figure in the practice of Christian spiritual direction today. Catholic spiritual direction finds many methods and many intellectual homes, from the great founders of spiritual families—Dominic, Francis, Ignatius—to newer ways of understanding and speaking about living the Christian life.

Today, in many parts of the world, spiritual direction per se has grown to embrace all religious traditions (and sometimes no tradition), as witnessed by the expansion of the U.S.-based organization Spiritual Directors International (SDI), initiated at a 1986 meeting of spiritual directors at the Sisters of Mercy Center in northern California and now incorporated in the state of Washington. On its website, SDI now claims some 6,600 members representing more than fifty traditions in forty-two countries.[1] The secretary of SDI is a lay ecclesial minister at a Catholic parish in Minnesota, and Catholics are well-represented on the editorial review panel for its journal, *Presence*. The membership of many Catholics in SDI, especially many Catholic women, points

---

1. See https://www.sdiworld.org/.

in another direction and underscores a basic fact: the Catholic Church does not ordain Catholic women to ministry. It appears that nearly half of the SDI membership identifies as offering Christian spiritual direction, and anecdotally a significant portion of these members are Catholic women.

Even though SDI does not endorse or certify spiritual directors, it remains the largest membership organization for directors and serves as both a virtual and real gathering place, as well as an educational resource. Membership alone imparts a kind of status.

Importantly, SDI has published "Guidelines for Ethical Conduct" in spiritual direction, and it recommends what it terms an "Engagement Agreement" for its members to use with their directees. The agreement stipulates the parameters of direction meetings (typically monthly, for one hour) to examine the directee's spiritual life, confirms that it is neither psychotherapy nor a means to financial advice, affirms the strict confidence in which direction conversations are held, presents a fee schedule, and asks for timely notice of cancellations.[2] SDI's professional training seminars often touch on the boundary issues that can arise in any ministerial relationship.

Other organizations, networks, and universities offer training in spiritual direction and in the supervision of directors. Many are Ignatian in focus, such as the Murphy Center for Ignatian Spirituality at Fairfield University, Connecticut, which offers a two-year weekend program for training spiritual directors, and the Office of Ignatian Spirituality, which operates online from various locations and connects Ignatian programs and retreat centers along the East Coast of the United States.[3]

---

2. A sample Engagement Agreement can be found at https://www.sdiworld .org/sites/default/files/find-a-spiritual-director/2012.11.21%20Sample%20 Engagement%20Agreement.pdf.

3. See https://www.fairfield.edu/catholic-and-jesuit/murphy-center-for-igna tian-spirituality/ and http://jesuitseastois.org/aboutus.

A BRIEF HISTORY OF SPIRITUAL DIRECTION

For Christians, Jesus is the first and, really, only companion in the life of the Spirit. In addition to Christ's teachings, which form the bedrock of the spiritual life, we find in Scripture others who accompany people in the Christian life. The epistles of St. Paul, who himself was brought to understand God's call by another disciple, Ananias, have multiple examples of spiritual wisdom. From the early Church, the writings of the desert fathers and mothers present even more advice on the spiritual life, and the *Sayings of the Desert Fathers* are as on point today as in the first few centuries of Christianity. While the fourth and fifth centuries produced more spiritual writing by men, most especially by the monk John Cassian, women now remembered as desert mothers also provided spiritual guidance to seekers. It appears at least a portion of the 1,202 sayings in the *Apophthegmata Patrum*–the *Sayings of the Desert Fathers*—can be traced to women. Known as *ammas* (the fathers were *abbas*), these desert mothers presented earthly wisdom, often commonsensical, to seekers. Perhaps the best known among the desert mothers is Amma Syncletica of Alexandria, but others remembered in the *Sayings* are Amma Sarah of the Desert and Theodora of Alexandria.

Theodora's story is both interesting and prescient. She disguised herself as a man to join a monastery, only to be discovered as a woman after her death. An example of her spiritual direction:

> She [Theodora] also said that neither asceticism, nor vigils nor any kind of suffering are able to save, only true humility can do that. [She told this story:] "There was an anchorite who was able to banish

80

the demons; and he asked them, 'What makes you go away? Is it fasting?' They replied, 'We do not eat or drink.' 'Is it vigils?' They replied, 'We do not sleep.' 'Is it separation from the world?' 'We live in the deserts.' 'What power sends you away then?' They said, 'Nothing can overcome us, but only humility.' 'Do you see how humility is victorious over the demons?'"[4]

Theodora's advice is as particular and personal today as it was centuries ago. The intervening years welcomed the wisdom of many women, and many of them were deacons.

There are women who served as deacons throughout the early centuries of the Church, in Syria, Palestine, Constantinople, Bithynia and Pontus, Cappadocia, Caria, Cilicia, Galatia, Lycaonia, Lydia, Phrygia, Italy, Egypt, Macedonia, Dalmatia, Moesia, Achaia (Greece) and the Greek islands, Africa, Gaul, and Pisidia.[5] There are deacon-abbesses from the early Church through the Middle Ages—Macrina and Olympias come to mind—but eventually the juridical position of abbess overtook the sacramentally recognized role of deacon.[6] Even so, later and even late in the West, there are many abbess-deacons, from Radegund, who founded the Abbey of the Holy Cross in Poitiers in the sixth century, to Heloise, whom Abelard called deacon in the twelfth.

As monastic life for women grew and formalized, prioresses and abbesses documented the spiritual advice they gave

4. The Patristics Project, https://www.patristics.co/sayings/.

5. See Ute E. Eisen, *Women Officeholders in Early Christianity: Epigraphical and Literary Studies*, trans. Linda Maloney (Collegeville, MN: Liturgical Press, 2000) and Kevin Madigan and Carolyn Osiek, *Ordained Women in the Early Church: A Documentary History* (Baltimore and London: John's Hopkins University Press, 2005).

6. Teresa Joan White, "The Development and Eclipse of the Deacon Abbess," *Studia Patristica*, vol. 19, ed. Elizabeth A. Livingstone (Leuven: Peeters Press, 1989), 111–16.

their sisters. Hildegard of Bingen, Beatrice of Nazareth, Gertrude the Great, and Teresa of Avila are joined by foundresses: Jane Frances de Chantal, Mary Ward, Elizabeth Bayley Seton. So, too, are the writings and advice of Catherine of Siena, Jeanne Marie Guyon, Edith Stein, Dorothy Day, Jessica Powers, and Ita Ford illustrative of predominantly informal spiritual direction given by women.[7]

The spiritual advice given by women, first offered by desert mothers and by women deacons, then later by abbess-deacons, was offered to the secular lay faithful as well as to early virgins and widows, to nuns and sisters. Whether from the remembered sayings of *ammas* (or *abbas*, from Anthony the Great, Pachomius, or John Cassian) to the great spiritual writers of today, the process of spiritual direction is and can be well-engaged in by women trained and often certified as spiritual directors by one or another program, whether university- or retreat center–based.

CONTEMPORARY SPIRITUAL DIRECTION

Today, although there are many schools and styles of spiritual direction, Ignatian spiritual direction has perhaps the clearest explanations and boundaries. Based on the *Spiritual Exercises* of St. Ignatius of Loyola and augmented by his writings, Ignatian spiritual direction has as its goal the freeing of the individual to live his or her life in God's care, accepting and cherishing the ability to see God in all things. The process is the acceptance and internalizing of the lifelong living of Ignatius's "Suscipe" prayer:

---

7. Phyllis Zagano, *Woman to Woman: An Anthology of Women's Spiritualities* (Collegeville, MN: Liturgical Press, 1993).

Take, Lord, and receive all my liberty,
My memory, my understanding,
And my entire will,
All I have and call my own.

You have given all to me.
To you, Lord, I return it.

Everything is yours; do with it what you will.
Give me only your love and your grace,
That is enough for me.

This prayer, which sums up the entire process, is given at the end of Ignatius's *Spiritual Exercises*.

Iñigo López de Loyola (1491–1556), a son of minor nobility in the Basque territory of northern Spain, is now remembered as the founder of the Society of Jesus, the Jesuits. His biography, written many times over, complements the autobiography he dictated in 1553 to his Jesuit secretary, Gonçalves de Câmara.

Iñigo Latinized his name to Ignatius as he began his ministry, apparently to make it easier to understand by people outside Spain. His early life as a courtier brought him an understanding of vanity; his injury as a soldier at the Battle of Pamplona in 1521 had brought him months of recuperation and reflection in his family's castle. His interior conversion during his recuperation there began his understanding of the ways of the human heart and led to a longer time in solitude, where he developed the *Spiritual Exercises* for which he is known.

By 1540, this debonair courtier-turned-mystic had gathered about him companions who eventually became priest-missionaries, vowing complete obedience to the pope in all things. When he died sixteen years later, there were more than one thousand members of the order. Both the *Spiritual Exercises* and the Jesuit *Constitutions* received papal approval before his death.

The practice of making the *Spiritual Exercises* has waxed and waned during their long history. At their most basic, they can be understood as Ignatius's methodology of teaching prayer to the uncatechized peoples of his territory, where priests were uneducated and often derelict even in celebrating sacraments. The Basque *seroras* mentioned earlier were well-known to Ignatius. He had at least one relative among them and resided with two *seroras* (rather than at his family's castle) during his final trip home before his priestly ordination.[8] The ministry of the *seroras* included much-needed catechetical instruction and, at least, informal preaching to the people of Basque Country, ill-served as they were by clergy.

Ignatius set out to rectify that need elsewhere in the world.

That women religious and secular women, reminiscent of the *seroras* whose ministry Ignatius apparently admired, have taken up his (and their) works of catechesis and spiritual direction cannot be ignored. Beginning in the 1970s in the United States, Jesuit retreat houses began training and adding women religious (often only one per center) to their permanent staffs. Women and men were able to experience the *Exercises* in many ways: during what often is termed the "long retreat" (typically a thirty-day period of deep silence), during a full eight-day retreat, or during the "retreat in daily life"—the "Nineteenth Annotation," by which Ignatius makes allowance for individuals who cannot separate from their worldly affairs. This last retreat can be completed in approximately thirty

---

8. Juan Garmendia Larrañaga, "El Señor de Loyola, patrono de la iglesia de San Sebastían de Soreasu y sus filiales. Las seroras (S. XVI)," *Boletín del Real Sociedad Bascongada de los Amigos del País* 63, no. 2 (2007): 471-81; and *AHPG-GPAH*, 2-0002, parte 1, fol. 154r. (I am grateful to Amanda Scott for this citation.)

weeks. Whereas in earlier times the retreats were preached, now the practice of individual spiritual direction in retreats has become popular, affording women, especially women religious, an opportunity both to minister and be ministered to by women. Some women's institutes, such as the Religious of the Cenacle, began offering individually directed thirty-day retreats in the early 1970s.[9]

The genius of the *Spiritual Exercises* is that its goal is the freeing from all unnecessary attachments. Through the four "weeks" of the exercises, the retreatant is first brought to the understanding of self as both created and redeemed; second, the retreatant is invited to choose a positive means of following Christ; third, the retreatant is guided to recognize the cost of discipleship; and, finally, the retreatant is encouraged to experience, cherish, and rejoice in the recognition of his or her true self and true vocation.

For the past fifty years or so, especially in the United States, religious and secular women have made the *Exercises*, have been trained as directors, and, more recently, have been trained as supervisors of individuals who direct the *Exercises*. The phenomenon has not always been met with accolades. I recall overhearing an elderly Jesuit at a retreat house in the eastern United States saying that it was not a "real" retreat house because it was overrun by women. (At the time, women directors were in equal or greater numbers on staff, there was a robust training program, and significant numbers of women and men came there to make eight-day and thirty-day retreats.)

Questions arising in the minds of many women about the wisdom of their seeking direction from a man combines with the increase in the numbers of women spiritual directors. During the past fifty years or so, especially in the United States,

---

9. *Cenacle News* 3:13 (September 30, 1971).

women spiritual directors (mostly women religious) began ministering to women outside the novitiate or formation setting, but from within their own religious houses. Today, as the first generation of women spiritual directors (most of them women religious) retires, their places are being taken by secular women, equally trained for ongoing individual directing and for retreat work.

But these secular women, unless they work in parish settings or in retreat centers, do not have the misused but implied "certification" of religious vows. Hence, the expansion of organizations like Spiritual Directors International, as well as various certificate training programs in spiritual direction.

CONFESSION

Spiritual direction is not confession, but as the women of the Church grow increasingly restive, their attendance to the sacrament of reconciliation has fallen away. The reactions of women to the prospect of confessing one's sins to a man range and rage: it is unnecessary; it is demeaning; it is dangerous. The often visceral and angry reaction of women to this sacrament, which some argue is made unnecessary by the penitential prayers of the Mass, collides with many other issues of interest and import to women. Even so, the sacrament of penance or reconciliation, "confession," has roots in Scripture.

James, "servant of God and of the Lord Jesus Christ," presents interesting advice in his epistle, the Book of James, written "to the twelve tribes in the Dispersion" (Jas 1:1). Discussions of authorship and exact dating of the work aside, we can recognize James's advice regarding what modern eyes can see as the confession of sins, "Therefore confess your sins to one another, and pray for one another, so that you may be healed" (Jas 5:16). The practice of confessing to elders was known in James's time, but the innovation referred to by James broadens the possibility of speaking with a contemporary.

Without doubt, the Catholic practice of sacramental confession finds its roots in the words attributed to Jesus: "If you forgive the sins of any, they are forgiven them; if you retain the sins of any, they are retained" (John 20:23). In 1151, the Fourteenth Session of the Council of Trent, which took place in northern Italy between 1545 and 1563, ruled that sacramental confession to a priest alone stems from the time of Jesus:

> If anyone denies that the sacramental confession was instituted, and is necessary for salvation, by Divine Law; or says that the manner of confessing secretly to a priest alone, which the Catholic Church has always observed from the beginning and still observes, is at variance with the institution and command of Christ and is a human invention, *anathema sit.*

Clearly, the Tridentine statement above, especially "the manner of confessing secretly to a priest alone, which the Catholic Church has always observed from the beginning" is problematic. But the words attributed to Jesus in the Gospel of Matthew can support the institution of the sacrament during his lifetime: "I will give you the keys of the kingdom of heaven, and whatever you bind on earth will be bound in heaven, and whatever you loose on earth will be loosed in heaven" (Matt 16:19) and "Truly I tell you, whatever you bind on earth will be bound in heaven, and whatever you loose on earth will be loosed in heaven" (Matt 18:18). The first statement, addressed to Peter, is enlarged by the second statement, addressed to the others. So the practice of confessing one's faults to another, here to an elder or to a chosen disciple of Christ, maintains an ancient heritage if not precisely according to the terms set out by Trent. Also, there is no mention of penance here in Matthew, even though reparation is clearly suggested elsewhere in Scripture.

The early Church did witness public confession and public reparation for sins, but the introduction of private reconciliation is credited to missioner monks from the East, who first brought the practice to Europe and, by the sixth or seventh century, to Ireland. Their understandings of spiritual direction, inherited from the *abbas* and *ammas*, traveled with them. From as early as the sixth century, up through the twelfth century, monks inhabited the barren rocks of the island of Skellig Michael, southwest of Kerry, Ireland. As in the practice of the desert fathers, an older monk would guide a younger monk in the spiritual life. The Irish term, *anam cara* or "soul friend," encompasses the spiritual relationship between the two. The younger monk would naturally discuss personal faults and failings with the older monk in private, to the point of giving a confession of sins. Recommendations both to recompense for and to overcome whatever moral failings the penitent suffered would be offered, again privately, by the senior monk. The recommendations grew to what today is termed penance, but only after a long period of change. People from areas surrounding Skellig Michael, and other monastic foundations, also engaged in the practice of seeking spiritual guidance from the monks, and the recompense for failings the monks recommended was commonsense reparation, so much so that Celtic law incorporated it. The monks also recommended what Ignatius would recommend later: *agere contra*, acting contrary to whatever sinful (or otherwise negative) inclination beheld the soul friend or penitent.

The practice of confessing one's sins privately developed among European monasteries as well. For nuns, the giving of spiritual direction and providing other formative processes were within the purview of the abbess who, at least until the later Middle Ages, was commonly also a deacon. So, too, was the receiving of confession of sins within the purview of the abbess-deacon. In fact, monastic rules sometimes included the directive that the abbess would hear the confessions, not only of the women in her monastery, but of the people in its surrounding territory. But the practice of seeking spiritual guidance, confessing one's sins, and receiving a necessary penance (again, as recompense for or as a means of acting against a given tendency, or both) eventually were both conjoined and separated in the early medieval Church.

The practice of confessing to an abbess was widely known, beginning at least in the seventh century. In the monastery of Brie, southeast of Paris, confession was made three times daily to the abbess, who had the power to excommunicate.[10] The rule for the nuns at Besançon (St. Joussan's), founded by Donatus in 624, included the requirement for regular confession to the abbess.[11] Also, the seventh-century *Regula cuiusdam ad virgines* provided that the abbess was authorized to confess the sisters and to delegate other sisters in her stead.[12] Note that the abbess's power of delegation underscores the fact of her juridical authority.

Abbesses could give spiritual guidance and receive and absolve the sins of others, but as their territorial authority was increasingly challenged, so was their ability to recommend penance and therefore their ability to forgive sin. The practice of women, in these cases territorial abbesses, offering reconciliation conflicted with the authority of bishops, who during the early medieval period increasingly challenged the rights of abbesses and abbots within their own abbatial territories.

---

10. Mary Bateson, "Origins and Early History of Double Monasteries," in *Transactions of the Royal Historical Society* 13 (London: Printed for the Society, 1899), 151.

11. Bateson, "Origins and Early History of Double Monasteries," 153.

12. Bateson, "Origins and Early History of Double Monasteries," 155.

Hence, medieval challenges to anyone other than a bishop offering penance (and therefore a judgement of reconciliation) begin to appear in the seventh century. As Theodore, archbishop of Canterbury, wrote in the late seventh century, it is "the function of the bishops and priests to prescribe penance."[13] Even so, the function had been granted to deacons as early as the third century under Cyprian, and up until the eleventh century either a priest or a deacon could officiate in the absence of the bishop.[14]

Further, it is generally recognized that confession to deacons (including deacon-abbesses) and to laity continued at least until the twelfth century, when the number and definition of sacraments was set, and even later in some places.[15] For example, on learning that in Spain Cistercian abbesses were hearing confessions of the sisters in their monasteries, the powerful Pope Innocent III, who reigned from 1198 to his death in 1216, forbade it, marking perhaps the definitive end to confession (arguably sacramental) to a woman in the Latin Church.[16] As Mary Schaefer points out, the late twelfth-century decision to finally fix the number of sacraments at seven and the 1215 Lateran Council decree requiring Eastertide confession to the parish priest combined to push older practices aside.[17]

---

13. Gary Macy, *Treasures from the Storeroom: Medieval Religion and the Eucharist* (Collegeville, MN: Liturgical Press, 1999), 173-74.

14. Henry C. Lea, *A History of Auricular Confession and Indulgences in the Latin Church*, vol. 1 (New York: Greenwood Press, 1968), 56.

15. Lea, *Auricular Confession*, 1:222-26; Mary M. Schaefer, *Women in Pastoral Office* (New York: Oxford University Press, 2013), 164.

16. Lea, *Auricular Confession*, 1:218, citing Cap. 10 Extra Lib, v. Tit. xxxviii; see Gary Macy, *The Hidden History of Women's Ordination: Female Clergy in the Medieval West* (New York: Oxford University Press, 2008), 102-3. "We are not a little amazed that abbesses...bless their own nuns, hear their confessions of sins of these same and, reading the Gospel, presume to preach publicly....We order you [bishop] to prevent [these actions]" citing *Corpus Iuris Canonici*, Decretales l. 5, t. 38, c. 10, ed. E. Friedberg (Graz: Akademische Druk, u. Verlagsanstalt 1959), 2:886-87.

17. Schaefer, *Women in Pastoral Office*, 164.

Concurrently, restrictions against deacons granting absolution grew, although historians generally find that "extreme necessity" justified admission of the sacrament by deacons. The 1196 Council of York forbids deacons permission to administer penance except in grave circumstances, soon defined by the Council of London as unavailability of a priest or in danger of death. The French theologian Peter Cantor (d. 1197) had opined that powers of absolution might be granted to deacons by the pope. There is contemporaneous mention in the Decretals of Gregory IX (ca. 1235) of confession to a priest or deacon.[18]

By the thirteenth century, as historian Henry C. Lea notes, "the formula of absolution became an absolute assertion of sacerdotal control over pardon," even as theologians contested the change in formula for the practice that eliminated the laying on of hands, signifying the invocation of the power of the Holy Spirit.[19] Therefore, the function and practice of confession with penance morphed over centuries from a wholly spiritual practice to one that was more juridical, and the juridical authority for it rested in the bishop.

Throughout ensuing centuries, however, the practice of confessing to a layperson continued to be supported in various ways by theologians, who argued positively or negatively regarding the sacramental value of such confessions, whether mortal or only venial sin could be considered, and whether the ministry of a priest was required for true absolution and reconciliation. The examples given often involved battlefield and deathbed circumstances, with laymen receiving the confessions of the injured and dying.

As acceptance of the sacramental character of the practice grew and strengthened, so did restrictions against deacons administering the sacrament. When viewed alongside

---

18. Lea, *Auricular Confession*, 1:57.
19. Lea, *Auricular Confession*, 1:52.

the increasing strength of the practice of the *cursus honorum*, restricting diaconal ordination to those destined for priesthood, the denial to deacons of the sacramental authority to forgive sins wanes and then falls under the strength of multiple legislations. While in the thirteenth century Bishop William of Paris recommends that a learned deacon hear confessions and determine penances when the priest is ignorant, various prohibitions against deacons granting absolution grew until bulls of Gregory XII (1574), Clement VIII (1601), and Urban VIII (1628) finally forbade the practice.[20]

The trajectory of law restricting confession and absolution is clear. At first connected to the spiritual direction of souls and practiced by monks, abbesses, and secular laypersons, during the twelfth century and following, bishops and priests claimed the juridical authority over the increasingly legally defined sacrament. The practice of the laying on of hands as a healing gesture fell away as the rubrics for the sacrament became formalized. What spiritual direction was available to the faithful was often adjunct to a judgmental act connected to ecclesial authority.

Following Trent, confession became highly regularized, as evidenced by the late sixteenth-, early seventeenth-century papal bulls noted above. As the practice of the sacrament became more regularized, the practices of spiritual direction and confession became entwined. The development moved in two directions: first, spiritual direction increasingly fell within the province of men only; and, second, theological principles

---

20. Lea, *Auricular Confession*, 1:374; 58-59, citing Gregor. PP. XIII. Const. 21, *Officii nostri*, August 6, 1574 (Mag. Bullar. Roman. II, 415); Clement. PP. VIII. Constit. 81, *Etsi alias*, December 1, 1601 (Bullar III. 142); Urbani PP. VIII Constit. 79, *Apostolatus officium*, March 23, 1628 (Bullar. IV. 144); Cf. Marc. Paul. *Leonis Praxis as Litt. Maior. Poenitentiar.* Mediolani, 1665, p. 297. Ferraris, Prompta Biblioth. s.v. *Absolvere*, Art. 1. N. 58, 59.

were enfolded into the practice such that discussion focused on the moral life as it related to the commandments.

Hence, women were left only the option of speaking with a man about their interior lives, their spiritual relationships with God, self, and others. For the most part, except within monasteries, women were bereft of feminine spiritual direction. The only option was the perfunctory and juridical experience of the confessional.

Today, many women find it difficult to engage in the practice of sacramental confession for these most obvious reasons. As they share their sad-hilarious "confession stories," the pain of abandonment is evident. For example, the woman who unburdened a tragic situation received in response: "Say three 'Hail Marys' and leave the door open when you leave." The woman who fearfully returned after many years was interrupted during her confession as the priest received a cell phone call. The woman who tearfully confessed one afternoon, the next day met her priest-confessor who announced loudly, in the center aisle of the church, "Well, you certainly look better today." The stories do not suggest that all priests are hopeless, but the stories do multiply. They are women's stories.

WOMEN'S STORIES ARE IMPORTANT

Why women spiritual directors? The answer runs in two directions: one, of course, is the ministry to women by women; however, second is the fact of women's skills and talents. While the term "feminine genius" coming from a pope[21] or another male cleric can be grating, when properly and respectfully

---

21. "Our time in particular awaits the manifestation of that 'genius' which belongs to women....The Church gives thanks for all the manifestations of the feminine 'genius,' which have appeared in the course of history." John Paul II, Apostolic Letter, *Mulieris dignitatem* (August 15, 1988).

understood, it can support the ministry of women. At the base of the need for women spiritual directors, and for women in ministry elsewhere, is the notion—the fact—that often women better receive other women's stories. Specific ministry to women by women—official ministry of women to women—ratifies the notions that both women and women's stories are important.

The ministry of women to women in spiritual direction returns to the earliest intent of the Gospel. The earliest mention of one-to-one reconciliation in the Letter of James is a healing ministry, not a juridical act. Hence, the practice of spiritual direction by women for women underscores several points:

> *First,* the history of spiritual direction and confession has roots in the specifically lay ministry of desert mothers and fathers.
>
> *Second,* while the practice of confession and consequent absolution at first was within the purview of men and of women, of deacons as well as of priests, it gradually changed to a juridical function controlled by the bishop, eventually delegated only to priests and not deacons.
>
> *Third,* the modern practice of the sacrament of reconciliation is distinct from the ministry of spiritual direction.
>
> *Fourth,* women increasingly are restoring themselves to the ministry of spiritual direction, yet predominantly with only tangential relationship to the Church as ad hoc ministers, often in private practice or working from convents and retreat centers of women's religious institutes.

Even so, throughout history, women have ministered to other women. We know that women deacons and abbesses especially ministered to other women. Often, this generally misunderstood fact is seen as a restriction and is given as a reason not to restore the Church's tradition of ordained women deacons. Yes, women deacons in history ministered to other women and men deacons primarily ministered to men. Who ministers to women today?

These facts and that question cannot too often be repeated. Opportunities for women to speak to women can be difficult to find. While there are many trained women spiritual directors, aside from ministries owned and operated by women religious, as noted above there are few places for full-time ministerial employment for secular or religious women. For the most part, women directors have found or made ad hoc arrangements for office space and insurance to practice spiritual direction outside of retreat centers and parishes. Sometimes they minster within their own convent spaces, sometimes in universities or divinity schools. Women trained in spiritual direction also obtain additional competencies in hospital or university chaplaincy, and their membership in certifying organizations attests to their competence and training. But on the parish level, where salary and funding support diocesan ministry, there seems to be only one parish in the United States, in Pennsylvania, that employs a layperson, a woman religious, as a permanent spiritual director. In short, the hierarchical Church neither regularly nor directly provides ministry by women to women.

Yet, women's stories are important, and the importance of women-to-women spiritual direction is documented in literature and borne out in contemporary practice. Even though confessing of sins is not part of spiritual direction, the impetus to share one's sin history is felt often and deeply by anyone making a directed retreat and often by individuals in ongoing spiritual direction. At the beginning of Ignatius's *Spiritual Exercises*, Ignatius presents the "Daily Particular Examination of Conscience." The book of the *Spiritual Exercises*, which is a manual for the director, presents three daily opportunities for an examination of "conscience," as Ignatius terms it, or of "consciousness," as the Jesuit George Aschenbrenner calls it.[22]

At the time he wrote his now-famous article, Aschenbrenner was director of novices at the Jesuit novitiate in Wernersville, Pennsylvania, a suburb of the city of Reading, approximately seventy miles west of Philadelphia. His explanation of the consciousness examen returns the practice to the roots of spirituality and spiritual direction and away from preparation for confession. As he states at the onset, "Examen must be seen in relationship to discernment of spirits. It is a daily intensive exercise of discernment in a person's life."[23]

The examination of conscience recommended twice daily by St. Ignatius can devolve to a recitation of the day's good and bad acts. Too often, the examen collapses to preparation for confession, leaving aside the crucial element of the discernment of spirits. Yet an investment in the realm of life-giving choices frees the individual to recognize his or her own talents and abilities, as well as unfree choices that tend to deaden the spirit. Such becomes the content of spiritual direction. While spiritual direction conversations can include recognition of sin and sinful tendencies, formal participation in regular spiritual direction can serve the ancient healing intent James's letter recommends and often bring it about.

The confession of sin is not formally part of spiritual direction, but the acknowledgment of sinful tendencies, even of sinful behavior, can form substance for the spiritual direction conversation. The equivalent of "penance" here would be solid advice, something more helpful than "say three 'Hail Marys' and leave the door open when you leave."

---

22. George Aschenbrenner, "Consciousness Examen," *Review for Religious* 31, no. 1 (January 1972): 14–21.

23. Aschenbrenner, "Consciousness Examen," 14.

WOMEN DEACONS AND SPIRITUAL DIRECTION

So, what about women deacons? What difference would it make if a qualified woman spiritual director were an ordained deacon? Again, the question reverts to the history of auricular confession.

Over the centuries, the practices of reconciliation, absolution, and the imparting of penance collapsed and became codified into the sacrament as defined by Peter Lombard around 1150 and affirmed by later theologians, popes, and councils. Importantly, the sacrament came to be inextricably connected to the "power of the keys" given by Christ to the Church but increasingly restricted first to bishops and then, by delegation, to priests.

In Matthew 16:19, Christ is quoted as saying to Peter, "I will give you the keys of the kingdom of heaven, and whatever you bind on earth will be bound in heaven, and whatever you loose on earth will be loosed in heaven." Matthew 18:18 repeats the authority earlier given to Peter to bind and to loose: "Truly I tell you, whatever you bind on earth will be bound in heaven, and whatever you loose on earth will be loosed in heaven." By popular understanding, the phrase grants the apostles and their successors the ability to forgive sins, although significant scholarship argues that only authority over excommunication is granted here, again to bishops.

John 20 is more explicit. After the resurrection, Jesus appeared to the apostles (less Thomas) through locked doors and said, "Peace be with you. As the Father has sent me, so I send you" (v. 21). And "when he had said this, he breathed on them and said to them, 'Receive the Holy Spirit. If you forgive the sins of any, they are forgiven them; if you retain the sins of any, they are retained'" (vv. 22–23).

Again, the consequent question remained as to whether the mission and the ability to forgive was given only to the apostles or they received these on behalf of the whole Church. We know, of course, that the early history of what eventually became the sacrament of confession or reconciliation included participation by laymen and laywomen, by monks and nuns, by deacons and priests, as well as by bishops. As the centuries rolled by, the increasing assertion of juridical authority by bishops and priests not only eliminated laypersons from the ministry of reconciliation but also removed a significant portion of the ministerial function from what became an increasingly juridical (and judgmental) practice. Wide discussion intent on separating what came to be called venial and mortal sins focused on judgement. Confessors' manuals surfaced, each focusing on the number and types of transgressions. Soon, the sacrament became a visit to the seat of judgement and not a participation in the healing ministry of Christ through the Church.

During the early eleventh century, a penitential in English (the *Late Old English Handbook for the Use of a Confessor*) comprised several manuscripts, variously presenting the confession ritual, a formula with a list of sins and petition for forgiveness, general directions, commonly focused on the major points: proper form for confession and specific penances relative to specific sins.[24]

In the late twelfth century, among the first medieval confessor's manuals, Alain of Lille's *Liber poenitentialis* was known in France, Belgium, the Netherlands, and the Holy Roman Empire.[25] Its 177 pages are divided into four parts, which (1) instruct the priest-confessor on his conduct and questions to

---

24. See "A Late Old English Handbook for the Use of a Confessor," ed. Roger Fowler, *Anglia* 83, no. 1 (1965).
25. Alan of Lille, *Liber poenitentialis*, ed. Jean Longere (Louvain: Editions Nauwelaerts [Analecta Medievalia Namurcensia 17], 1965).

ask, (2) present the requirement that he emphasize contrition on assigning penance, (3) consider the possibility of solemn public penance, and (4) advise on further procedural matters.

As the practice of jurisdictional remission of sins with a judgement of guilt, again, as opposed to ministerial reconciliation with a response aimed at healing, progressed, the practice of naming and controlling indulgences arose.

INDULGENCES

There are varied roots to the Catholic understandings of indulgences. In the early Church, those facing martyrdom could apply their pain to others' penitential debts. For some time, the debate was whether indulgences would be applied to owed penance or to temporal punishment (time in purgatory) after death for sins committed in life, including those sins forgiven through confession and sacramental absolution.

During the Middle Ages, complicated formulae arose allowing for the performance of certain actions abating or eliminating assumed (future) time in purgatory, and as the years progressed, numerous abuses arose, including the sales of indulgences. While the Fourth Lateran Council (1215) attempted to suppress the abuses, they tended to grow unabated and were a driving force of the Protestant Reformation. Martin Luther railed both against the fact of indulgences (by implication always for sale) and even the right or ability of the pope to grant them. By the time of Trent, to meet Protestant complaints, the assertion arose that indulgences stemmed from the time of the apostles.

However, the developed theory of indulgences is essentially post-Trent, and the various theories surrounding indulgences begin to codify with the Tridentine reforms. In fact, the final session of the Council of Trent found and defined that the Church's ability to levy indulgences came from Christ.[26] The complicating factor in the theory of indulgences is that it competes with the theology surrounding the remission of sins through sacramental confession and absolution. Some theologians argued that the ancient practices of confession and attendant penance were not sacramental, thereby requiring further recompense for sin. In any event, older theories of indulgences vary, but maintaining the same underlying notion: Only the hierarchical Church had control over remission of sin, penance, and, apparently, postmortem punishments. By the time of Trent, women were no longer within the ambit of those who would or could hear confessions and levy penances and so certainly could not have any authority over indulgences.

Independent of the theological, even historical, arguments about indulgences, which continue to this day, the ministry of healing the self-inflicted wounds of sin morphed into a juridical exercise, complete with a penitential sentence and subsequent postmortem debts, all controlled by clerics. The understanding carried over to the sacraments ministered by those attending to the ill and dying.

---

26. Lea 2:4n4, cites C. Trident. Sess. XXV. Contin. Devr. De Indulgent: "Quum potestas conferendi indulgentiae a Christ Ecclesiae concessus sit...;" Council of Trent, Twenty-Fifth Session, Concerning Indulgences: "Whereas the power of conferring indulgences was granted by Christ to the Church..."

5
ANOINTING OF THE SICK

> There are deaconesses in the Church, but they are not assigned priestly tasks....Their ministry is performed solely among women and its purpose is to safeguard decency, so that men who perform sacred rites do not see the body of a woman when unclothed at the moment of baptism, when her virginity must be certified and on the occasion of care of the sick.
>
> Epiphanius, *Pan.* 79.3.6–4.1

T HE PRACTICE OF ANOINTING ill persons is known early in Christianity and earlier in the ancient world. Known as the "oil of faith" in the first-century Jerusalem *Lamina* and the "mystery of the candlestick" among Syrian Maronites, the earliest documents term the practice and the sacrament "anointing of the sick" and, later, "extreme unction."[1]

As the Gospel of Mark reports, the apostles were missioned to a healing ministry by Jesus: "They cast out many

---

1. Andrew J. Cuschieri, *Anointing of the Sick: A Theological and Canonical Study* (Latham, MD: University Press of America, 1993), "Introduction" and pp. 1-15.

demons, and anointed with oil many who were sick and cured them" (6:13). If we consider the "demons" the tendencies for or the remnants of sin, then in Mark we can see a connection between healing from physical ills and remission of sins.

Later, the connection between sin and sickness, long understood as definite in the ancient world, is solidified in the Letter of James. Sick persons, benefiting from the prayer of the church's presbyters, will be saved and their sins forgiven:

> Are any among you sick? They should call the elders of the church and have them pray over them, anointing them with oil in the name of the Lord. The prayer of faith will save the sick, and the Lord will raise them up; and anyone who has committed sins will be forgiven. (Jas 5:14–15)

The practice of anointing ill persons with blessed oils is further rooted in the above section of the Letter of James. Anointing had two aims: the healing of physical ills and the healing of spiritual ills. Today, only a man ordained as priest may offer the sacrament of the sick.

Was it always this way? Did women participate in this very beautiful and very necessary sacramental act of healing and forgiveness? Did women ever anoint ill persons?

In truth, the people of the early Church benefited from anointing by many persons, notably through the ministrations of St. Geneviève (fifth to early sixth centuries), patron saint of Paris. But as the sacrament's definition solidified, only clerics were permitted to anoint.[2] Even so, the healing ministries of women for women are recorded in Scripture and in history.

We know as well that women anointed other women in baptism. The ancient ritual called for whole-body anointing,

---

2. Thomas M. Izbicki, "Saint Geneviève and the Anointing of the Sick," *The Catholic Historical Review* 104, no. 3 (Summer 2018): 393-414.

done only by women for women. Recall, women accompanied, directed, and confessed other women. The intimate details of a woman's relationships with God, self, and others were (and still are) more properly discussed with another woman. It follows, therefore, that the custom of anointing ill women would fall to women, especially women deacons.

French Cardinal Jean Daniélou, SJ (1905–74), a *peritus*, or expert adviser, at the Second Vatican Council, contends that by the third century, the order of women deacons had "inherited" the pastoral duties of the order of widows (which order had begun to include the oddly termed "virgin-widows"). As Daniélou puts it, these inherited pastoral duties included visiting the sick. Citing the early third-century *Didascalia Apostolorum* (XVI, 135), which was modeled on the earlier (perhaps first-century) *Didache*, Daniélou finds that women deacons attended to ill women living in non-Christian houses. More importantly, Daniélou argues that the later (fourth-century) *Apostolic Canons* match the descriptions of the earlier *Didascalia*: women ministered to ill women.

That is, Daniélou finds that the early Church evidences an ordained order of women deacons that performed ministerial duties. With the evidence of the fifth-century Council of Chalcedon, Daniélou submits their ordinations are real: "It is not just a question of any sort of laying-on-of-the-hands, or of a blessing."[3] Chalcedon's canon 15 states clearly that a woman may not be ordained under forty years of age, and the term used is the technical term for ordination: *cheirotonia* (χειροτονία), the laying on of hands. The women were ordained to their ministry.

Which brings us back to the sacrament for the sick.

Daniélou reviews the findings of Epiphanius, bishop of Salamis in Cyprus, a fourth-century doctor of the Church known for fighting heresies. In his *Against Heresies*, Epiphanius

---

3. Jean Daniélou, *The Ministry of Women in the Early Church*, trans. G. Simon (Leighton Buzzard: Faith Press, 1974), 22 from *La 'Maison-Dieu* 61 (1960).

dealt at length with the question of women and priesthood and argued strongly against women partaking of any specifically priestly ministries. He may, in fact, be the first to suggest that because Jesus did not select Mary, his mother, to replace Judas as an apostle, therefore women could not be ordained as priests.[4] That aside, Epiphanius did find that propriety dictated that women—and only women—would anoint other women or even visit them in their homes. Epiphanius further argued that women, if they belonged to a Church order, only belonged to the order of deacon and that they assisted priests and bishops in the performance of their ministries.[5] That is, women were not in the order of presbyter, nor could they perform priestly duties, but they were in the order of deacon. Epiphanius implies that ministry to the sick and dying, including anointing, was not a presbyteral task. Further, as Daniélou points out, the ministry to sick women, especially including the laying on of hands, could not be performed by a male. Therefore, Daniélou asks, "Ought we not then to think that in fact it [the sacrament of the sick] was administered by the Deaconesses?"[6]

If we agree with Daniélou, then three areas of discussion ensue: (1) the relationships between healing and forgiveness in the context of the sacrament; (2) contemporary understanding of and administration of the sacrament of the sick; and (3) the place of the sacrament in view of the participation of women in health-care chaplaincy and ministry to the sick and dying.

HEALING AND FORGIVENESS

The theological connection between healing of physical ills and the remission of sins is both tenuous and strong. The relationship

---

4. Epiphanius, *Against Heresies* 79.3.
5. Epiphanius, *Against Heresies* 78.13.
6. Daniélou, *Ministry of Women*, 28–29.

is tenuous, as two clearly distinct and, at least in contemporary thought, unrelated things take place: healing and forgiveness. The relationship is strong because at least one of the healing miracles of the Gospels includes the explicit remission of sin.

Consider, for example, the healing miracles at the beginning of Mark's Gospel: the man with a skin disease (Mark 1:40–45), the paralyzed man (Mark 2:1–12), the man with the paralyzed hand (Mark 3:1–6), the hemorrhaging woman (Mark 5:25–34), Jairus's daughter (Mark 5:21–42), the deaf mute (Mark 7:31–37), and the blind man (Mark 8:22–25). Of these, only the paralyzed man in Mark 2, whose friends lowered him into the house where Jesus was teaching, is first told that his sins are forgiven.[7] The others are cured and healed, but there is no mention of sin. Such is an important point, because the ancient belief that physical infirmities were evidence of prior sinful behavior would cause the acts of healing and forgiveness to be conjoined.[8] The inherited belief is so strong that, as in the case of the paralyzed man in Mark, sins would necessarily be forgiven before any physical cure could take effect.

When we examine the history of the sacrament of the sick, as it is now known, we can see its evolution from an action intended to heal the body to one that necessarily includes the healing of the soul to one that requires juridical authority to remit sin. As others have pointed out, the systematization of the seven sacraments by the early Scholastics required them to account for the facts of healing actions of saints who were not clerics, somehow "distinguishing it from sacramental ministry, although both types of healing involved divine action through the person anointing."[9]

---

7. The concept is clearer in Mark: "When Jesus saw their faith, he said to the paralytic, 'Son, your sins are forgiven'" (2:5); whereas Luke reports, "When he saw their faith, he said, 'Friend, your sins are forgiven you'" (5:20).
8. Exod 20:5; Deut 5:9; also, Luke 13:2; John 5:14; John 9:2.
9. Izbicki, "Saint Geneviève and the Anointing of the Sick," 393-94.

WOMEN: ICONS OF CHRIST

By the twelfth century, both Peter Abelard (1079–1142) and Hugh of St. Victor (1096–1141) found the act of anointing had two ends, healing and remission of sin, leading to their determinations that the only proper minister of anointing was a priest (or bishop), given anointing's juridical result and the fact that it was generally offered only in expectation of death. By the end of the twelfth century, the sacrament was termed extreme unction, at least in the West. The Scholastics differed on the sacrament's spiritual effects, bickering over whether actual sin or only its unhealthy remnants were removed following anointing, and by the thirteenth century, they reignited the discussion of who might administer it. Here, again, the focus was on the act of anointing, not as a ministration for illness, but rather as a healing from sinful acts and actual remission of sins in preparation for death. Coincidentally, lay confession was falling out of favor, so deacons were more rarely delegated to grant absolution and anointing, which by this time generally required a priest.[10] Then, the continued clericalization of the sacrament through the Middle Ages led to the 1614 decree of Pope Paul V systematizing the ritual and ruling it could be performed only by a priest.

The Council of Trent decreed the sacrament of extreme unction was "alluded to by Mark but recommended and promulgated to the faithful by James." Trent defined the sacrament as one that forgives sin and "at times when expedient for the welfare of the soul restores bodily health."[11] The conciliar documents, however, refer only to the "proper minster" of the sacrament. That is, Trent does not appear to decree that

---

10. Izbicki, "Saint Geneviève and the Anointing of the Sick," 396, citing Andrew Cuschieri, *Anointing the Sick: A Theological and Canonical Study* (Langham, MD: University Press of America, 1993), 38–42.

11. Council of Trent, Fourteenth Session, November 25, 1551; *De Extrema Unctione*, cap. 3 and canon 4. See also Denz.-Schön. 1697 and 1719; and *Code of Canon Law*, canon 1003.

a deacon cannot administer the sacrament of the sick (by then called extreme unction); it simply reserves its administration to a "proper minister."

Who might that be? The history of the sacrament keeps it within the purview of deacons, even allowing it to be performed by laypeople in times of necessity.[12] But by the time of Trent there were precious few people who lived a diaconal vocation permanently. The 1917 *Code of Canon Law* stipulated and decreed that only a priest could administer the sacrament validly, thereby connecting liceity with sacramental validity. That is, in the 1917 *Code*, the law defined its validity.

When the 1917 *Code* was being modified, there was an attempt to remove the codification of what constituted validity from the first paragraph of the canon on extreme unction, as well as an attempt to remove the stipulation that the action may be performed *omnis et solis* by a priest. Later changes to Canon Law did not affect the law on anointing and canon 1003 para. 1 of the 1983 *Code* nearly replicated canon 938 para. 1 of the 1917 *Code*. That is, the determination that only priests and bishops may anoint remains: "Every priest and a priest alone validly administers the anointing of the sick."[13]

Such is the current state of the law regarding the sacrament of the sick. And the law effectively eliminates the historically documented tradition of deacons and laypersons administering the sacrament, even despite wide discussion about restoring deacons to its named licit and valid ministers. The difficulty with canon 1003, as it stands, is that its determination of validity appears to depend on the facts of its liceity; if it is not legal it is invalid. The canon further presumes that only

---

12. For several centuries, a great part of the discussion focused on the response of Pope Innocent I (378-417) to Decentius, which some argued allowed laypersons (male or female) to anoint.

13. See John P. Beal, James A. Coriden, and Thomas J. Green, eds., *New Commentary on the Code of Canon Law* (Mahwah, NJ: Paulist Press, 2000): 1185-86.

priests who have the "care of souls" oversee the sacrament's administration to those in their care. That is, the juridical position of the priest or bishop is considered, be they legitimately appointed abbots, bishops, pastors, chaplains, or others who exercise *cura animarium*—"the care of souls."

Because the discussion now is not historical, that is, because the current discussion is really about who can perform the sacrament of anointing, it is useful to look at the actual liturgies. We can and must note especially that there are three forms: (1) simple anointing, (2) a liturgy of anointing within a Mass, and (3) a liturgy of anointing with communion. The rite of reconciliation, if requested, is a separate and distinct event.

THE SACRAMENT OF THE SICK

There are three presenting questions regarding the sacrament of the sick. First, is remission of sin an effect of the sacrament of the sick in the same way the remission of sin is an effect of the sacrament of baptism? Second, if remission of sin is an effect of the sacrament of the sick as in baptism and not the result of a juridical act, why is the licit and valid administration of the sacrament of the sick formally restricted to priests, while not granted to deacons? Finally, if remission of sin is an effect of the sacrament and not the result of a juridical act, why is the administration of the sacrament of the sick not permitted to laypersons in the case of emergency, as with baptism?

It seems that the main distinction between the remission of sin through baptism and the remission of sin via the sacrament of the sick is that the latter sacrament can be repeated, as with other sacraments whose graces are understood to bring healing and consolation: reconciliation and Eucharist. That is, baptism belongs to the category of nonrepeatable sacraments, which includes confirmation and holy orders, whereas the sacrament of the sick, reconciliation, and the reception of Eucharist can and often are repeated. But repeatable or not, the sacraments of the sick and baptism both remit sin.

The defined history and practice of baptism allows it to be administered by any person in time of dire necessity, even as it can be and often is later formalized (but not repeated) by a priest in a church, during which ceremony the newly baptized is anointed. Can the same argument be made for the sacrament of the sick? That is, in the case of emergency, can the sacrament of the sick be offered by nonpriests in its first ritual formula, without any previous or attendant juridical act? Such a determination would allow for simple but sacramental anointing by deacons and laypersons, especially deacons and laypersons who serve as hospital, hospice, and nursing home chaplains.

Pastoral Care of the Sick: Rites of Anointing and Viaticum, the manual for performing the sacrament approved for use in the United States, notes, "If necessary, the sacrament also provides the sick person with the forgiveness of sins and the completion of Christian penance."[14] That is the only reference to the remission of sin. "If necessary" would lend a position of urgency to the administration of the sacrament, especially in emergency situations. So why can only a priest anoint ill persons?

To investigate the possibility of an expansion of the ability to sacramentally anoint, that is, for persons who are not priests to licitly and validly anoint the sick, independent of and separated from the rite of reconciliation, is to look toward

---

14. *Pastoral Care of the Sick: Rites of Anointing and Viaticum* (New York: Catholic Book Publishing Corp., 1983), 21, citing Session Fourteen, Council of Trent and Denz.-Schön. 1694 and 1695. The manual comprises the English-language rituals from the *Roman Ritual* as revised by the Second Vatican Council and published as *Ordo Unctionis Infirmorum eorumque pastoralis curae* in 1973.

the restoration of the sacrament of the sick to the ministry of the deacon and, in this case, the ancient and documented ministry of women deacons.

The instructions for the rite make it clear that, while "minister," "deacon," and "priest" are mentioned within it, the terms and therefore the roles are not interchangeable. That is, all actions may be performed by priest, some also by deacons, and some also again by "ministers," here understood as laypersons, most probably lay ecclesial ministers.

In its most basic form, the sacrament itself is simple. The minister (again, in current law only a priest) anoints the head and hands of the ill person, saying while anointing the forehead,

"Through this holy anointing may the Lord in his love and mercy help you with the grace of the Holy Spirit."

And, while anointing the hands:

"May the Lord who frees you from sin save you and raise you up."
The response to each prayer is "Amen."[15]

The administration of the sacrament of the sick can be contained within a eucharistic or noneucharistic liturgy. The rubrics for its administration outside the Mass include introductory rites, sprinkling with holy water, a general penitential rite (without individual confession, which is recommended to be offered prior to and separately from the liturgy), a Gospel reading, followed by the "Liturgy of Anointing," which comprises a litany of prayers, a silent laying on of hands, the blessing of oil, the actual anointing as described above, and

---

15. *Pastoral Care of the Sick*, 111.

attendant prayers. If the sick person is to receive communion, the liturgy continues as would a communion service. With or without communion, there is a concluding rite and a blessing.

To be sure, there are parts of the ritual that can be performed only by a cleric—deacon, bishop, or priest—but there are none that seem (theologically, at least) reserved to priests or bishops. Yes, the real or assumed care of the individual is required, and that reverts to the bishop, pastor, or head of a household of religious (typically understood as a house of religious clerics). But the entire liturgy, whether in its most basic form, in an expanded form, or including a communion rite, includes nothing outside the deacon's charge or ministry.

Except, the actual anointing is said to remit sin and the Church teaches that only a priest may do so. But the *Roman Missal*, as translated and adapted, makes it quite clear that reconciliation is separate and distinct from the act of anointing, and specifies that a separate and distinct sacrament should be offered outside the liturgy of the sacrament of the sick. By analogy, if the simple or solemn baptizing with water performed by a layperson or deacon is sufficient to remove sin and its remnants, should this not be the case for the simple anointing by a deacon or even by a layperson in case of emergency?[16]

The most recent definitive note regarding the sacrament of the sick came from the Congregation for the Doctrine of the Faith in 2005 and is signed by Cardinal Joseph Ratzinger as prefect and Archbishop Angelo Amato, SDB, as secretary, with an accompanying letter by Ratzinger and an unsigned commentary.[17] The Note is neither a decree regarding a disciplinary matter nor an instruction clarifying law. Neither is it a

---

16. Some diocesan bishops, where their episcopal conferences have agreed, have requested and received rescripts for lay ecclesial ministers of their choosing to solemnly baptize and to witness marriages.

17. Congregation for the Doctrine of the Faith, "Note on the Minister of the Sacrament of the Anointing of the Sick" (February 11, 2005).

declaration, nor an authentic declaration, nor a response to a *Dubium*. Neither is it a doctrinal note, as the 2002 CDF "Doctrinal Note on Some Questions Regarding the Participation of Catholics in Political Life."[18]

The Note is merely headed Note, without qualification. The Note states that, following the *Code of Canon Law* (c. 1003), the *Code of Canons of the Eastern Churches*, the Council of Trent, and the *Catechism of the Catholic Church*, "only priests (bishops and presbyters) are ministers of the anointing of the sick" and that the doctrine (as defined by Trent) is to be held definitively:

> This doctrine is *definitive tenenda*. Neither deacons nor lay persons may exercise the said ministry, and any action in this regard constitutes a simulation of the Sacrament.[19]

The tenor of this 2005 Note is much like that of the joint Notification issued in September 2001 by the Congregations for the Doctrine of the Faith, for Divine Worship, and for Clergy, which stated that because the Church does not foresee ordination of women as deacons, it is therefore illicit "to prepare women candidates for diaconal ordination."[20] That Note quite probably forced the creation of Roman Catholic Womenpriests, begun with priestly ordinations on a Danube riverboat on June 29, 2002, and preceded one day earlier

---

18. Congregation for the Doctrine of the Faith, "Doctrinal Note on Some Questions Regarding the Participation of Catholics in Political Life" (November 24, 2002).

19. "Note on the Minister of the Sacrament."

20. "Notificatzione delle Congregazioni per la Dottrina della Fede, per il Culto Divino et las Disciplina dei Sacramenti," per il Clero, September 17, 2001. The document was signed by the prefects at the time: now-retired Cardinals Joseph Ratzinger (CDF) and Jorge Arturo Medina Estévez (Divine Worship) and deceased Dario Castrillón Hoyos (Clergy).

by diaconal ordinations on land.[21] Anecdotally, it is thought that at the time some of the seven German-speaking women, including one woman from the United States, were preparing for the diaconate under the guidance of their bishops.

DEACONS AND WOMEN IN CHAPLAINCY

Hospital, nursing home, hospice, and home-care chaplaincy have increasingly become the provenance of lay chaplains, especially of women chaplains. Founded in 1965, the National Association of Catholic Chaplains (NACC), a membership organization of nearly 2,000 individuals (837 male, 1,113 female), oversees avenues for Clinical Pastoral Education Certification and for ongoing professional education.

The NACC defines its member chaplains as "Roman Catholics who manifest proficiency in Catholic theology and spiritual care praxis...[whose certification is determined] through written materials and an in-person interview."[22] Certification is open to Roman Catholics or members of Churches in union with Rome[23] who have an accredited graduate-level theological degree in addition to a bachelor's degree and four units of Clinical Pastoral Education (CPE) accredited by the Association for Clinical Pastoral Education (ACPE) and the responsible agency of the U.S. Conference of Catholic Bishops (USCCB/CCA, Commission on Certification and Accreditation) or the Canadian Association for Spiritual

---

21. Phyllis Zagano, *Women & Catholicism: Gender, Communion, and Authority* (New York: Palgrave MacMillan, 2011), 98–104.

22. See https://www.nacc.org/certification/board-certified-chaplain/.

23. The NACC website lists only fourteen of the more than twenty such churches and lists several other churches and communions excluded from membership, although it reports sixty to seventy-five non-Catholic members.

Care (CASC/ACSS, Association canadienne de soins spiri-
tuels). The USCCB created its subcommittee for approving
Clinical Pastoral Education and ministry formation programs
in 1982.

Why all this? Like Spiritual Directors International, the
NACC is a relatively new organization that professionally
certifies individuals for specific ministries. No doubt, specific training is needed for both spiritual direction and for
health-care chaplaincy, but the phenomenon of professional
certification for each challenges the fact of ordination. In the
contemporary Church, many Catholics may be less likely to
accept the ordained status of an individual (particularly that
of a priest) as a qualification or certification for health-care
chaplaincy and be more likely to accept the ministry of a certified lay minister or deacon. In fact, health-care chaplaincy
has become so specialized that there is a clear distinction
between priests and others who are CPE trained and certified,
and there are specific subspecialties within the field. That is,
the sacraments attendant to health-care chaplaincy (reconciliation and anointing) are respectfully considered, but the ability to administer them is not significantly required for either.

So, what does it mean to minister to ill and dying persons? Who is best suited to accompany the sick? It is here that
the diversion between the historic ministry of anointing ill
persons and the formalized sacrament of the sick create a sort
of cognitive dissonance within the believing Church. Many different individuals minister to the sick. Family and friends, certainly, join physicians, nurses, and other hospital employees
whose comfort and ministrations form a circle of care around
the patient.

Enter the chaplain. In the United States, the NACC counts
353 priests, 61 deacons, and 370 women religious among its
2,000 members. Secular lay ministers make up its majority
membership. Many Catholic and other health-care agencies

and hospitals provide Catholic chaplaincy services. These range from chaplains' visits to patient rooms and a dedicated chapel, to regular or occasional celebration of Eucharist, opportunities for reconciliation, and bedside administration of the sacrament of the sick. For whatever reasons, and there are many, in too many settings the ministry of a priest is perfunctory and relatively anonymous. That is, the staff chaplain—more often a layperson or deacon—will have accompanied the ill person. But when the time for the sacrament of the sick comes, a priest arrives to administer the sacrament. Unfortunately, the priest is too often someone who does not know the ill person. The situation is complicated by the historical facts of priests assigned to hospital ministries in the United States, often the last stop for an incompetent or accused priest and now too often the purview of immigrant priests with minimal cultural understandings and language abilities.

The question about the administration of the sacrament of the sick resounds in hospitals and nursing homes: Why are certified Catholic chaplains not able to anoint?

Clericalism is a facile but real answer. The history of women anointing ill women is clear. Today, of course, there is no real restriction to women anointing, excepting that their doing so would not be sacramental and, indeed, a certified Catholic chaplain (or spiritual director) would never want to appear to be simulating a sacrament. In some settings, the lay ecclesial minister or deacon certified as a chaplain will accompany the priest, introduce him to the patient, and sometimes join in or add to the priest's anointing.[24]

---

24. Catholic chaplaincy certification is fraught with canonical questions due to canons 654-57 and the 1997 Instruction "On Certain Questions Regarding the Collaboration of the Non-Ordained Faithful in the Sacred Ministry of Priests," which restricts the term "chaplain" to priest. An accommodation reached with the USCCB in 2004 allows the NACC to "issue the certification of 'chaplain' for the sake of 'the profession' for the hiring institution." See Bishop Dale J. Melczek, "Use of Title 'Chaplain' in Pastoral Care Ministry," NACC, https://www.nacc.org/

WOMEN: ICONS OF CHRIST

There is another objectively serious complication. Picture an ill and dying woman who has been accompanied for weeks or months by a woman chaplain. Now, helpless in her home or hospital bed, she finds a strange man touching her, rubbing oil on the palms of her hands. Such can be a startling and, in some cultures, a very offensive act. There are obvious reasons to explain why monastic women deacons were responsible for anointing their ill sisters and, in some times and places, even laypersons within their territories.

Which returns us to the question of lay anointing. It is generally understood that anointing by a priest or layperson (and, presumably, by a deacon) was an accepted practice that waned and finally died out during the time of the Carolingian reform, from the mid-eighth through the mid-ninth centuries.[25]

Prior to that evaporation of the generally accepted practice of lay anointing, Decentius, the fifth-century bishop of Gubbio in northern Italy, wrote to Pope Innocent I (d. 417) asking about various liturgical matters. One was about the sacrament of the sick. The pope's response was twofold: priests may absolve individuals in danger of death; priests and laypersons are permitted to anoint ill persons with oils consecrated by the bishop. That later theologians, canonists, even popes did not counter Innocent's opinion (could it be considered an instruction?) marks the acceptance of the custom but does not clarify whether the anointing could be considered sacramental.[26]

Has Innocent's determination been overcome by default?

vision/most-requested/use-of-title-chaplain-in-pastoral-care-ministry/. In the United States, only the Archdiocese of New York refuses to participate in this accommodation.

25. Cuschieri, *Anointing of the Sick*, "Lay Anointing," 17–29.

26. Cuschieri, *Anointing of the Sick*, 18n56 refers to Leo the Great, *Codex Canonum Ecclesiasticorum*, Captit. XXIII, cap. 8 coll. 517–518 and Benedict XIV *De Synodo Dioecesana Libri Octo. Romae*, 1748, Lib. VII, cap. 19, n. 1, p. 309.

Innocent's response clearly allows for lay anointing.[27] Just as with baptism, could current discipline allow the emergency administration of the sacrament in its simplest form (and even with Viaticum) by a lay minister or deacon recalling the canonical stricture regarding the individual priest or bishop holding *cura animarum*?

---

27. Innocent I's responses to Decentius of Gubbio's fifth-century questions regarding liturgy include the possibility of lay anointing. Specifically, Innocent wrote that priests absolve only the Thursday before Easter or when individuals are near death, and that both priests and laity may anoint the sick. Paul Turner, "The Amen Corner: Between Consultations and Faithfulness; Questions That Won't Go Away," *Worship* 89, no. 4 (July 2015): 351–58.

6

CONCLUSIONS

I will stand at my watchpost,
    and station myself on the rampart;
I will keep watch to see what he will say to me,
    and what he will answer concerning my complaint.

For there is still a vision for the appointed time;
    it speaks of the end, and does not lie.
If it seems to tarry, wait for it;
    it will surely come, it will not delay.

Habakkuk 2:1, 3

WHERE DO WE GO FROM HERE? The history of the diaconate—male and female—is clear. The needs of the ancient and medieval Church dictated the ways the diaconal ministry evolved, expanded, and contracted. That women deacons existed cannot be denied, nor can their participation in sacramental ministry. That women were ordained at the altar during Mass, in the presence of other deacons and presbyters, by bishops in liturgies that included the *epiclesis*, during which they self-communicated from the chalice and received a stole from and were called deacons by the ordaining bishop, supports the fact that their ordination can be considered sacramental.

The ministries of the ordained women deacons of the past, from their assisting at baptisms and catechizing new Christian women and children, to their somewhat limited abilities to preach and proclaim the Gospel, to their altar service and subsequent banning from the sanctuary, to their juridical authority for reconciliation and their providing spiritual companionship and direction, to their ministries to the sick and dying (including anointing) underscore the possibilities for today's renewed diaconate.

We know what women deacons did. Can we imagine what they could do in and for the Church today? The question is not one of functionality. The question is one of the Church proclaiming the Gospel in a new-old way. Beneath every objection to restoring women to the ordained diaconate is the suggestion that women cannot image Christ. Of course, women do not, cannot "image" the human male Jesus exactly. But the extraordinary fact of the Incarnation is that Jesus, God, became human. Women are human. And all humans are made in the image and likeness of God. The androcentric blind spot in theologies denying the ability of women to image Christ belie a naive physicalism embedded in arguments against the ordinations of women to any grade of order, including the diaconate.

History demonstrates that the early Church had no such difficulties with ordaining women or with women being near the sacred.

The first argument, against the possibility of women receiving the sacrament of orders, reduces to a less-than-human status for women. That less-than-human status for women is echoed in today's headlines, as women and girls are routinely disrespected, raped, trafficked, and murdered in every country of the world. Unless the Church allows itself to return to its historical respect for women, allows itself to once

119

again sacramentally ordain women, the tears, violations, slaveries, and deaths of thousands and thousands of women will be charged against it.

The second argument, against the possibility of women being near the sacred, divides. It is a basis for enforced clerical celibacy in the Latin Church, and it grows from the first argument, which denies the full humanity of women. The ancient taboos regarding blood and, consequently, menstruation join with unusual understandings about sexual relations and outrageous commentary about women to require women to keep their distance from the sacred and for men who touch the sacred not to be near women. As these taboos combined with the problems of nepotism and inheritances, celibacy became and remains the norm for Latin priests, although some leeway is allowed for married Protestant ministers who convert. The great majority of Eastern Catholic Churches, as well as those of Orthodoxy, retain the earlier tradition of married deacons and priests. (Both East and West maintain a requirement for celibate bishops.)

There is a deep need for Christian ministry around the world and a deeper need for the Church to recognize its past in preparation for its future. The discussion in this book points to the solution, not only for the needs of the Church, but for the ills of the world. The needs exist and so does the solution. There has never been a formal decree against women being ordained as deacons, nor can there be one, lest the Church deny its own history.

Will the Church restore its past in acceptance of its present and in preparation for its future? A simple *motu proprio* modifying a few canons in the *Code of Canon Law*, mainly for their pronouns, would allow the Church to move forward. Canon 1024 ("A baptized male alone receives sacred ordination validly.") could be modified to: "A baptized male alone receives sacred ordination as presbyter validly." Realistically speaking, that is what the original canon meant to say anyway, given the progressive codifications during the centuries as they kept in lockstep with the *cursus honorum*. Only men destined for priesthood could be ordained, including as deacons.

A simple *motu proprio* modifying canon 1024 and changing pronouns where they refer to deacons in fact is the logical next step to meet the Church's expressed desire to include half its members more fully in the Church's ministry and mission, not to mention its administration. The question of women deacons is a legal, not a doctrinal, issue, and the modification of the appropriate canons will allow the Church to provide for its pastoral needs. Without doubt, the needs of the Church universal must be addressed, but in a manner so that individual local churches are able make their own decisions based on their own needs. The point of this book has been to establish the facts and possibilities for the entire diaconate, which in its fulness can include both men and women. My hope is that the Church will recover its past, accept the present, and joyfully live a fully Christian future.